MAKING
TRACKS

MAKING
TRACKS

A WHISTLE-STOP TOUR
OF RAILWAY HISTORY

PETER SAXTON

Michael O'Mara Books Limited

First published in Great Britain in 2015 by
Michael O'Mara Books Limited
9 Lion Yard
Tremadoc Road
London SW4 7NQ

A CIP catalogue record for this book is available from the British Library.

Papers used by Michael O'Mara Books Limited are natural,
recyclable products made from wood grown in sustainable forests. The
manufacturing processes conform to the environmental regulations of the
country of origin.

ISBN: 978-1-78243-329-3 in hardback print format
ISBN: 978-1-78243-332-3 in e-book format

1 2 3 4 5 6 7 8 9 10

Jacket design by Patrick Knowles

Illustrations by Aubrey Smith

Designed and typeset by Design 23, London

Printed and bound by CPI Group (UK) Ltd, Croydon, CR0 4YY

www.mombooks.com

For my mother, who always believes in me.

CONTENTS

INTRODUCTION

R AILWAYS OCCUPY AN INTERESTING place in the public psyche. Endlessly complained about, discussed and used as an excuse for lateness in almost any circumstance, they are also loved, obsessed over and romanticized more than any other form of mass transport.

My own obsession, I am convinced, comes from my mother. Like many women today, although unlike a lot of women in the early 1960s, my mother continued working throughout her pregnancy. She would travel daily between our home in Wimbledon and her job as a cook in Sloane Square, bouncing on the springy cushions of the rattling, red-painted District line trains from the 1920s that were still doing sterling service at that time. After I was born, circumstances dictated that she had to return to work so she took me daily on the same journey right up until I started school. We would always (at my insistence) sit in the same seat, looking to the right so that I could gaze at the endless procession of main-line trains on the way to and from Waterloo. Trains that included fast, clattering expresses to Portsmouth; plodding, whining suburban sets that stopped at all stations to and from exciting day-trip destinations such as Chessington and Hampton Court; and, thrill of thrills, steam-hauled expresses bound for the Wessex coast. All painted the sober, attractive green that, quite frankly, is the colour trains should be.

I had no option other than to be completely hooked. Add to that a train-enthused father who would take me to the footbridge outside Wimbledon station to wave at the drivers (oh, the excitement of a wave back and sometimes a friendly toot) and you will understand that life conspired to make me a hopeless train freak.

This book is a brief history of railways and how different people came up with innovations and designs that cumulatively have led to the systems we have today. And how their individual genius combined in the one central genius – that of railways themselves.

BUILDING THE RAILWAYS

GAUGE MATTERS: OR 'WHY ARE THEIR TRAINS BIGGER THAN OURS?'

IN ITS SIMPLEST FORM, a railway track consists of a pair of rails, held parallel by a series of structures known in the UK as sleepers and in the US as ties. This track is generally laid on a bed of ballast although in some cases it is fixed directly on to a concrete base. This latter method is known as slab track; it needs less maintenance and is used principally in areas that have very high usage or that are tricky to reach, such as tunnels. The track is sometimes referred to as 'the permanent way'.

A railway gauge is, straightforwardly, the measurement of the space between the rails. The table on the next page shows some of the more commonly used gauges in the world.

Width between the rails	Used in
1,000 mm (metre gauge)	Brazil, Switzerland (many mountain railways), some African countries, south-east Asia
1,067 mm (3 ft 6 in)	Some areas of Australia, Indonesia, Japan (except high-speed lines, which are standard gauge), many African countries, New Zealand
1,435 mm (standard gauge) (4 ft 8½ in)	Most widely used worldwide (approximately 60 per cent of railways)
1,520 mm (5 ft)	Russia and some former Soviet states
1,600 mm (5 ft 3 in)	Ireland and some areas of Australia
1,668 mm (5 ft 5½ in)	Spain and Portugal (except high-speed lines, which are standard gauge)
1,676 mm (5 ft 6 in)	India, Pakistan, Argentina, Chile

LOADING GAUGE

The track gauge alone is not the sole factor contributing to the overall size of the trains running along it. The loading gauge is the measure that defines the maximum size trains can be in order to operate safely, taking into account bridges, tunnels, stations and other trackside structures. The British loading gauge, with some limited exceptions, is one of the tightest relative to track gauge – the British network, being the oldest in the world, is still suffering from the legacy of early mistakes and lack of central planning.

British rail users often return from continental Europe or the US raving about the wonders of double-deck trains and lamenting the lack of them at home. It is the loading gauge that is responsible; the continental, or Berne gauge, is much more generous than the UK's.

EARLY DAYS

The world's first modern, double-tracked, steam-hauled railway was the Liverpool and Manchester, opened in 1830. Prior to that, the Stockton and Darlington had opened in 1825, also using steam technology for some of the time. However, this had proved unreliable so horses were often used instead, harking back to an earlier age of wagonways in which wooden and later iron rails had been laid to enable horses to pull heavy loads out of mines. These would then be sent along to shipment points with much greater ease than if they had been transported across bare ground or deep mud.

The concept of using specific tracks or grooves wasn't new even then – the Ancient Greeks and Romans had dug out channels to help carts and wagons along their way without sliding. From the Middle Ages up to around the middle/end of the eighteenth century, both Germany and Britain had wagonways in their mining regions and the earliest rails (as opposed to grooves) appeared in Germany in the mid-sixteenth century.

Obviously it's impossible to keep vehicles on rails without some sort of controlling device. Early rails used flanges (raised ridges or rims) to ensure that wagons didn't veer off. These flanges were later transferred to the inner edges of the wheels themselves and it is this method that has survived to the present. The idea of using rails for transportation, therefore, wasn't new by the early nineteenth century, but advances in technology meant that railways were about to experience an explosion in popularity. Hitherto, horse – or indeed human – power was the main form of traction (although some employed cables or gravity) but it was the development of steam that really got things going.

The steam engine began as a stationary machine that was used to drive water pumps, but it wasn't long before enterprising engineers found a way to connect it to wheels and therefore become self-propelling. As with railways themselves, the idea of using steam power wasn't new, but it was in the early nineteenth century that the technology really took off.

RICHARD TREVITHICK

Steam-powered road vehicles had been attempted in the seventeenth and eighteenth centuries but it took Richard Trevithick, a mining engineer from Cornwall, to come up with the idea of running locomotives on rails. Previous engines had been far too heavy for the road surfaces of the period so rails were the answer. After much trial and error, in 1804 Trevithick demonstrated a locomotive at Pen-y-Darren, an ironworks in Merthyr Tydfil, South Wales. This machine got up to the dizzying speed of 8 km/h (5 mph). Later Trevithick demonstrated his locomotive, prophetically enough, near the site of the current Euston station in London, running it on a circular track and calling it 'Catch Me Who Can'.

Trevithick soon left England, however, and continued to develop steam engines (albeit stationary ones) in the mines of Peru, leaving the way clear for that first genius of the railways, George Stephenson.

GEORGE STEPHENSON

George Stephenson was born in 1781 at Wylam, Northumberland, not far from Newcastle. He became a pit boy at a local mine but began to educate himself in engineering skills with the help of a local schoolmaster. He moved to become an enginewright and found a job at Killingworth coalmine, looking after the stationary steam engines there. These engines were used to haul wagons up from the mines using cables and Stephenson soon came to realize that a more effective use of the power would be to run steam engines as moving locomotives. He set about designing his first creation and in 1814 it was unveiled as the locomotive *Blücher*. It has to be said that Stephenson's genius did not lie in his own inventions – he had incorporated a lot of Trevithick's ideas into his locomotive design – but more in his ability to adapt existing technologies in ways that made them hugely more efficient.

THE STOCKTON AND DARLINGTON RAILWAY

Stephenson continued to build engines – not always with success – and in the early 1820s he was approached by a group of businessmen from Darlington. They had had the idea of a railway line linking their collieries to the town of Stockton, at the mouth of the river Tees. Impressed by Stephenson's engineering to date, they asked him to become the surveyor and engineer of the route.

After overcoming fox-hunting landowners reluctant to see this new technology defiling their land, as well as calculating ways to cross rivers and a major swamp, Stephenson opened the Stockton and Darlington railway in just three years, on 27 September 1825. There was, however, a major issue. George Stephenson may have been a genius, but his early steam locomotives were prone to failures. He and his son

Locomotion No. 1

Robert had produced an engine for the opening of the line – *Locomotion No. 1* – but the mine owners were not convinced by its potential and continued to use horses for many of the trains until a new locomotive, designed by Timothy Hackworth from Stephenson's works, proved a greater success.

One Stephenson innovation on the Stockton and Darlington above all has proved an enduring success – his choice of rails set 1,435 mm (4 ft 8½ in) apart. This is the standard gauge adopted by most major railways throughout the world.

THE LIVERPOOL AND MANCHESTER RAILWAY

George Stephenson's next major project was to prove a turning point in the history of railways – the Liverpool and Manchester. This was a much bigger scheme than the Stockton and Darlington, linking as it did two major powerhouses of nineteenth-century British industry. And whereas the Stockton and Darlington was conceived as a predominantly freight railway (although it did end up carrying passengers),

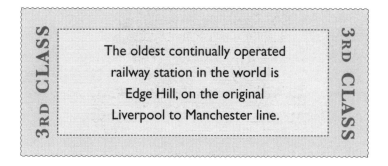

3RD CLASS

The oldest continually operated
railway station in the world is
Edge Hill, on the original
Liverpool to Manchester line.

3RD CLASS

the Liverpool and Manchester was planned as a route that would carry both freight and passengers.

As with the Stockton and Darlington Railway, this new route had its problems. Objections were raised by local canal owners (who could see their business disappearing to the new railway) and the terrain was tough. The river Sankey had to be crossed by a nine-arch viaduct and the high ground at Olive Mount in Liverpool had to have a 3.2 km (2 mile) cutting driven through it. The greatest obstacle, however, was Chat Moss – a huge area of peat bog that wouldn't take normal railway construction methods. Stephenson's solution was innovative – he floated the railway across the bog on a bed of tree branches and heather, bound with tar and covered with rubble. The Chat Moss line is still in use today – a testament to the genius of George Stephenson – and has recently been electrified.

Steam traction was still a controversial technology at that time so the directors of the line decided to run a competition to find the best engines of the age. This took place in 1829 at Rainhill near Liverpool and became known as the

2ND CLASS

The busiest railway station in Britain is London Waterloo – it also has the most platforms at twenty-four.

2ND CLASS

Rainhill Trials. There were five serious contenders – Robert Stephenson's *Rocket*, Timothy Hackworth's *Sans Pareil*, John Braithwaite and John Ericsson's *Novelty*, Timothy Burstall's *Perseverance* and Thomas Shaw Brandreth's *Cycloped*. *Cycloped* wasn't a steam locomotive but was powered by a horse on a treadmill – it was the first contender to withdraw after the horse fell through the floor. *Rocket* lived up to its name and won the day easily – none of the other entrants finished the course.

Unlike the Stockton and Darlington line, built as a single track with only a few passing places, the Liverpool and Manchester had been designed to be double track throughout – greatly helping capacity and reliability and eliminating the unpleasant stand-offs found on the Stockton and Darlington when trains in opposite directions encountered one another on the single track.

The Liverpool and Manchester opened on 15 September 1830. It was a hugely important day – the Duke of Wellington, the then Prime Minister, was in attendance, along with the great and good of both cities. Sadly, however, the day was spoilt by a tragic event. At a stop for the special opening locomotive to take on water, William Huskisson, MP for Liverpool and former cabinet minister, got off the train and walked down the track in order to speak to the Duke of Wellington. He failed to notice until too late that the *Rocket* was approaching on the other line. To the horror of the onlookers, he was struck by the locomotive and his leg was completely mangled. He was taken to hospital in Eccles on a train driven by Stephenson himself at speeds reaching a phenomenal (for the age) 56 km/h (35 mph). Nothing could be done, however, and Huskisson died that evening, thus becoming the first high-profile casualty on the railways.

Both George and Robert Stephenson went on to construct further railways, notably the much longer London and Birmingham line. George helped with the construction of early railways in Belgium and Spain and also advised on construction of some of the first railways in North America.

After a long career (and three marriages), George Stephenson died of pleurisy, aged 67, on 12 August 1848 in Chesterfield, Derbyshire.

ISAMBARD KINGDOM BRUNEL AND THE THAMES TUNNEL

The next great British railway genius was an engineer who overturned accepted norms and came up with a set of achievements unparalleled for the age.

Isambard Kingdom Brunel was born in Portsmouth in 1806, three years after the birth of Robert Stephenson. His father was the engineer Marc Brunel and together they worked on

Isambard Kingdom Brunel

Construction of the Thames Tunnel

the first tunnel under the Thames between Wapping and Rotherhithe – the first engineered tunnel under a navigable river anywhere in the world. Construction started in 1825 though floods, gas leaks and financial problems meant it didn't open until 1843.

The tunnel was constructed using a revolutionary new method known as the Shield. This was a large iron framework made of thirty-six individual chambers, each large enough to hold one workman, open at the back but with a wooden board at the front. The whole contraption was pushed into place against the earth to be excavated and each workman would remove the wooden board and proceed to excavate the earth in front of him. Once he had dug to the required depth, he would move the board to rest against the new earth face and ensure that the newly excavated cell was secured using props. Once all of the workers had completed their segment, the entire framework would be moved forward and the process would begin again. Behind the excavating team would be a band of bricklayers, busy constructing the line of the tunnels as the digging proceeded.

Originally conceived as a tunnel for horses and carts, it opened as a tourist attraction and thousands of people visited to walk through the colonnaded passageways. However, the

Clifton Suspension Bridge

tunnel gradually became the haunt of prostitutes and thieves and eventually, in 1865, the East London Railway bought it with a view to creating a rail link between east and south London. Brunel's tunnel today still sees intensive service as part of London's Overground network.

After working on the Thames Tunnel, the Brunels turned their sights to the competition to build a bridge across the Avon Gorge at Clifton, Bristol. Isambard's design for a suspension bridge won the day – at the time it had the longest span of any bridge in the world. Sadly for Brunel, though, investment for the bridge took a long time to come through and although construction started in 1831 it wasn't completed until 1864 – five years after his death.

BRUNEL AND THE GREAT WESTERN RAILWAY

Following Brunel's successful design bid for the Clifton Suspension Bridge, the board of the nascent Great Western Railway approached him to be their chief engineer. This line was to connect London to Bristol but, typically for Brunel, he had bigger ideas. He proposed that the Great Western Railway should provide a seamless journey all the way from London to New York, consisting of a train to a shipping terminal in Neyland, South Wales, and then a crossing of the Atlantic by his own steamer *Great Western*, all on one ticket.

One major and visible difference that Brunel brought to

the Great Western compared to the other railways springing up across the country was the track gauge. He chose his own broad gauge – 2,140 mm (7 ft ¼ in) – claiming that Stephenson's gauge was fine for mines and industry but that a fast passenger and freight railway would benefit from the stability and space afforded by his chosen dimensions. Unfortunately for broad gauge aficionados, the standard gauge took root quickly throughout the rest of the country, leading to chaotic scenes at stations where the two systems met, with passengers and their luggage struggling from one train to another. To help overcome this, large portions of the broad-gauge system were laid with dual-gauge track, allowing through-working from the standard gauge. However, the Great Western eventually bowed to the inevitable and converted fully to standard gauge. The last broad-gauge train ran in 1892.

Another Brunel invention failed because of a lack of suitable materials. For the Great Western's extension from Exeter to Plymouth, Brunel decided to try a method of propulsion known as the atmospheric railway. Where a standard railway would use moving locomotives, an atmospheric railway uses a vacuum system, where stationary pumps suck air from a pipe in the centre of the track, thus drawing the carriages along. Square-towered pumping stations were built at two-mile intervals (one can still be seen at Starcross on the estuary of the River Exe). Initial results were reasonable enough – trains ran up to 109 km/h (68 mph). However, vacuums need to be sealed effectively and at the time the way to do this was by using leather flaps. Leather didn't hold up very well in the extremes of weather and the tallow used to keep it supple attracted rats. Their constant gnawing meant that a seal became impossible without constant maintenance, so the bold atmospheric railway managed to run for less than a year in 1847–8.

Of course, glitches aside, Brunel's legacy of success is all around – from the design of Paddington and Temple Meads stations in London and Bristol respectively, to Box Tunnel between Bath and Chippenham (at the time the longest railway tunnel in the world) and the Royal Albert Bridge crossing the River Tamar between Devon and Cornwall. Special mention too for the Maidenhead Railway Bridge: because Brunel wanted to keep his Great Western Railway as level as possible (it was nicknamed 'Brunel's Billiard Table'), he needed to find a way of spanning the Thames at Maidenhead without creating a bridge with a hump in

THE STATION WITH THE LONGEST NAME IN BRITAIN IS

LLANFAIRPWLLGWYNGYLLGOGERYCHWYRNDROBWLLLLANTYSILIOGOGOGOCH

IN ANGLESEY, WALES

it. His solution is still in place today – at the time the twin arches were the widest, flattest brick arches ever attempted. There is a widespread story that the Great Western Board didn't believe that such arches could stay up by themselves so they instructed Brunel to keep the scaffolding around the bridge in place. He agreed, but secretly had the scaffolding lowered so that it wasn't actually supporting anything. When the scaffolding was subsequently washed away in a flood, the bridge remained triumphantly standing.

Isambard Kingdom Brunel died of a stroke in 1859 and is buried in Kensal Green Cemetery, London.

THE EARLY YEARS OF BRITISH TRAIN TRAVEL

PEOPLE-CARRIERS: DEVELOPMENTS IN PASSENGER COMFORT

MOST PEOPLE, WHEN CONSIDERING railways as a form of transport, are concerned with such factors as the speed of the journey and the comfort of the accommodation on offer. The very earliest railways, when designing the first passenger-carrying vehicles, took their inspiration from the existing method of mass transport – the stagecoach. Coachbuilders had had many years' experience in constructing robust vehicles that would stand up to long journeys along appallingly maintained roads. In 1830, George Stephenson asked Thomas Worsdell, in business as a coachbuilder since 1813, to come up with a design for the carriages to run on the Liverpool and Manchester Railway.

Initial efforts were unstable. By 1838, however, Worsdell's son Nathaniel came up with the 'Enterprise' coach, in which three stagecoach bodies were fixed together and mounted on a single, four-wheeled chassis. This had the effect of creating a carriage with three closed compartments and set a trend for railway design that lasted right up to the 1990s when the last completely closed-compartment stock was finally withdrawn from the commuter lines in south-east London.

Old habits die hard, however, and the earliest carriages were still painted as if they were three separate stagecoaches, with curved lines demarcating each compartment. There was even a space on the roof for the guard, as in horse-drawn days, but it soon became clear that the increased speed of a train, plus the constant shower of soot and sparks, meant that separate accommodation elsewhere in the train had to be provided.

As in general life, the class system permeated the railways and therefore separate accommodation was provided for first-, second- and (reluctantly) third-class passengers. The precise accommodation on offer varied from company to company but first-class passengers received the greatest luxury, including windows and padded seats in their compartments. Second class might have padded seats but a window only in the door of the compartment. Third class started out as open carriages, akin to farm carts or goods wagons, crudely divided with wooden planks for seats. By 1844 it was realized that this latter form of transport was becoming unacceptable and Parliament compelled the railway companies to provide at least one train a day for third-class passengers to be made up of covered carriages.

PASSENGER COMFORT INCREASES

As the nineteenth century progressed, speeds increased and carriage design had to evolve to keep up. Four-wheeled carriages are all very well but they do not feel very stable or comfortable at higher speeds. In addition, there is a limit to how long they can be and railway companies were soon looking for ways to increase the number of passengers they could carry. Thus the bogie coach was born – the style of carriage that is most familiar today. A bogie is a framework carrying either four or six wheels situated at each end of the carriage, resulting in longer coachwork and a more stable ride for passengers.

As carriage design improved, the railway companies began to look at offering onboard services that would tempt people away from their competitors on long-distance routes. The enclosed stagecoach design clearly limited the ability of people to move around, and the need to add toilets and dining cars created further problems. Soon, therefore, the majority of long-distance trains were made up of carriages linked to one another by side corridors leading to individual passenger compartments. A variation of the theme saw the corridor running down the centre of each carriage, with seating either side. This is the layout in use today on most railways, although there are still side-corridor carriages operating in continental Europe and sleeper carriages generally preserve this layout to enable enough room for lateral beds.

Linked to the improved nature of carriage design was the improvement in conditions for third-class passengers. During the early years, third-class accommodation, although better than the original open wagons, was not even provided on many express trains – third-class passengers were expected to use the slowest trains on offer. The Midland Railway, however, decided that it would add third-class carriages to its network of express services – and while the accommodation was initially provided with hard wooden benches, this was soon upgraded to upholstery, giving a completely different experience to those without the means to pay for more expensive travel.

THE PULLMAN EXPERIENCE

The drive to improve onboard standards led to the first collaboration between a British railway company and an American company, the name of whose founder is even today a signifier of luxury travel.

George Pullman (1831–97) was an engineer, born and raised in New York State, who first made his name in Chicago. Here he helped with the immense project to install a sewerage system, involving the raising of the city by some 1.8–2.4 m (6–8 ft) above its existing position, using a system

Interior of a Pullman car

of jacks to raise individual buildings then constructing new foundations underneath.

He went on to design luxurious sleeping carriages for the railway, followed by stylish restaurant cars, providing the complete hotel experience on rails.

The general manager of the Midland Railway, James Allport, had visited the United States in 1872 in order to find out if there were any lessons to be learned with regard to improving service for his own passengers. Struck by the luxury of the Pullman carriages, he placed an order and the first Pullman entered service in the UK in 1874. Complete with attendants supplied by the Pullman Company, the accommodation was made available at a supplementary fare and quickly gained a reputation for offering standards of comfort, catering and service not previously encountered.

The concept spread to many other companies throughout the country, with the London Brighton and South Coast Railway being the first to offer a full Pullman train, between London and Brighton, from 1881. This was the start of a tradition that continued right the way through to 1972, when the last all-Pullman train on the route, the *Brighton Belle*, was finally taken out of service.

The *Brighton Belle* carried an illustrious clientele – when British Rail removed kippers from the breakfast menu, regular patron Lord Olivier led the protests.

A TOUCH OF CLASS

The Midland Railway was responsible for another major development in the extension of comfortable travel – in 1875 it abolished second class completely, bringing its third class up to the previous second-class standard. (The Parliamentary requirement to maintain third-class services meant that it was easier to stick with the denomination of third class rather than go through the effort of changing the law.) Other companies began to follow suit, leading to the situation in which the vast majority of trains in Britain carried first- and

THE GROUPING: BRITAIN, 1923

The Railways Act (also known as the Grouping Act) of 1921 was introduced to bring some order to, and to limit some of the losses being made by, the 120 or so private companies that had hitherto been running the railways in Great Britain. During the First World War the government had taken control of the railways in the national interest and full nationalization was considered for a time. The Railways Act was a compromise solution that ordered the multiple concerns into just four big, still-private railway companies.

Inevitably known as the Big Four, they were:
• The London, Midland and Scottish Railway (LMS)
• The London and North Eastern Railway (LNER)
• The Great Western Railway (GWR)
• The Southern Railway (SR)

The Big Four came into being on 1 January 1923, on which date all of the railway companies were subsumed into one of the four, apart from the railways we now know as the London Underground, some jointly run railways such as the Midland and Great Northern and the Somerset and Dorset, and a number of light railways that had sought and won an exemption from the Act.

third-class carriages, but no second class. This was rectified in 1956 when third was renamed second. And in turn, second was renamed standard class in 1987, removing the perceived pejorative overtones of the idea of 'second-class passengers'.

As an aside, one group of British trains that did retain second class up to the 1950s were the Boat Trains linking to the Continent. Continental railways maintained three classes of accommodation for a lot longer than in Britain, so some second-class coaches were kept available to maintain the ability to book an entire journey in the same class.

Coaching stock design remained fairly static once the general concepts of bogie coaches, corridors, onboard toilets, dining cars and sleeping cars had been put in place. The 1930s saw a period in which there was a renewed push to offer even more facilities on some trains – hairdressers, cinema coaches, observation cars – and clearly today we have air-conditioning and improved bogie design to allow faster, smoother running, but overall the basic layout of train carriages hasn't changed that much over the years.

EARLY RAILWAYS ON THE CONTINENT

BELGIUM

BELGIUM WAS AN EARLY adopter of railways. It had become
independent from the Netherlands in 1830 and thus,
as a brand-new country, took the view that it should
be in the vanguard of technological development. Unusually
for the early days in railways, which were generally seen as a
free-for-all for private industry, the Belgian state contributed
greatly to the development of the first lines. The first railway
in Belgium ran from Brussels to Mechelen and was opened
in May 1835 – the first railway in continental Europe.
Following this, the country developed a cross-shaped system,
with Brussels at its centre, connecting the other major cities,
ports, industrial areas and neighbouring countries. Because
of central government control there were no competing or

duplicated lines (as so often in Britain) so the whole system had efficiency built in from the start.

FRANCE

For a country that is now held up by some as a shining beacon of railways, the development of a national network in France took some time to get going. Generally less industrialized than Britain and with a better road and canal network, the impetus for railway construction just wasn't there in the early days. In addition to this, voices opposed to railways were stronger in France than in many other countries and the fact that the government was involved in railway policy (as France didn't have the industrial base that Britain did, there wasn't a core group of industrialists willing to fund railways) meant that an extraordinary amount of time was taken up with debating the issue, rather than planning the network and getting on with construction. By 1840, compared with 2,000 route miles in Britain, France had constructed only 350.

Eventually, the French government stepped up their efforts and provided facilities for the design and engineering of new railways. A substantial network quickly emerged, in which most lines operated radially from Paris to all parts of the country. This government control, however, meant that the concentration on Paris as the natural hub of the network ignored the fact that there was a need for transverse lines linking towns and cities away from the capital. This meant that in some cases, transporting materials by rail between towns only a hundred or so kilometres from each other meant a huge detour of hundreds more up to Paris then down again. This situation was broadly rectified as the network developed, but even today Paris is very much the centre of railway operations in France.

> When the Réseau Breton branch from Paimpol to Guingamp in Brittany was converted from metre to standard gauge, workers started at opposite ends of the line. Unfortunately they chose different sides of the track to lay the third rail ...

GERMANY

The political situation in Germany at the time of early railway construction couldn't have been more different to the centralized state of France. Indeed, there was no single German state but a collection of kingdoms, princely states and dukedoms, each with its own laws and customs, albeit bound together by a common German language. This disunity, however, did end up favouring the construction of a balanced network – without a recognized central hub such as France had in Paris, cities of roughly equal importance formed their own hubs around themselves.

The kingdom of Bavaria saw the first steam-powered

railway in Germany. Opening in 1835 between Nuremburg and Fürth, it covered a distance of 6.5 km (4 miles). The first trunk route opened four years later between Leipzig and Dresden (120 km or 75 miles). Seeing the success of the early railways, other German states began to build them, so that by 1845 the network had already reached 2,000 km (1,200 miles). And a network it was, crossing state boundaries and knitting together the disparate territories.

By 1846, the various railway companies had created an administrative union that regulated uniform fares throughout the network. The logical next step for a growing number of Germans was to take that concept and apply it politically, creating a unified state. This eventually happened after the Franco–Prussian War in 1871 with the proclamation of the Second German Empire under the Prussian king Wilhelm I.

SPAIN

The early days of Spanish railways are an object lesson in state isolationism and fear leading to long-term difficulties. The first stretch of track was opened between Barcelona and Mataró (a town 30 km or 19 miles north east of Barcelona) as late as 1848 – but what created the problem was the decision that Spanish railways should be built at a gauge of 1,668 mm (5 ft 6 in). The Spanish government was extremely concerned that using the standard gauge would make a land invasion by France much more likely. Therefore a change of gauge at the frontier would slow down any army, making the situation more favourable for the defenders. This invasion threat turned out to be illusory and Spain (and, by default, Portugal, which had gone along with the wider gauge rather than risk being stranded as a small island of standard gauge with no connections anywhere) was left with a network incompatible with the rest of Europe. This did, however, lead to exciting (to enthusiasts) scenes at frontier stations where through-carriages from France travelled slowly through a shed in which the axles of each carriage were unlocked and the wheels moved apart to adopt the wider gauge. Since 1992, Spain has embarked on a construction programme of high-speed lines (known as the AVE) that are built to standard gauge to enable through-trains to be run without the need for a gauge change.

SWITZERLAND

Given its pre-eminence in operating a public transport system today, it might be surprising to learn that Switzerland came rather late to the railway revolution. Up to the mid-nineteenth century it was a relatively poor country, with a disunited structure of government based on administrative districts known as cantons. And of course its territory largely consisted of huge mountains, inimical to early railway construction.

Following the construction of the first railway between Baden and Zürich in 1847, lines opened in the less mountainous regions over the next few years (to a network plan drawn up

Mountain train in front of the Matterhorn peak, Switzerland

in part by Robert Stephenson). As time went on, Switzerland began to industrialize and, with an eye on its position at the centre of Europe, realized that a railway line through the heart of its territory linking Germany in the north with Italy in the south could prove extremely lucrative. Supported both politically and financially by those two countries, a 15-km (9-mile) railway tunnel through the St Gotthard pass began construction in 1872, opening ten years later and proving an immediate success with freight streaming through. This provided the impetus needed for the development of the rest of the main Swiss network, including two further tunnels under the Alps – the Simplon and the Lötschberg.

Railways eventually criss-crossed Switzerland, including the many mountain routes so popular with tourists today. Electrification came early to the network, partly down to coal shortages but also thanks to the availability of hydroelectric power and the undoubted supremacy of electric traction over steam, especially in mountainous areas.

EUROPE (DIS)UNITED

By the late nineteenth century most of the main lines across Europe were in place, allowing easier transport than ever before, both for passengers and freight. This was the start of the great heyday of rail travel, with overnight sleeper trains linking cities across the continent. Of course this also provided an excellent network for moving troops and military equipment in case of war. Railways performed an essential role in both world wars, with all sides intent on protecting their own assets and destroying those of the enemy. In the Second World War, huge efforts were made by air forces on both sides to bomb railway networks, and nations poured massive resources into fixing their own lines as soon as possible after they were destroyed. In some cases, as part of a scorched earth policy, railways were deliberately destroyed by fleeing troops, who used massive rail ploughs to destroy wooden sleepers once the last evacuating train had passed along.

THE *ORIENT EXPRESS*

As international rail lines proliferated, a network of overnight trains carrying sleeping cars was developed. The most famous of these, the *Orient Express*, linked Paris and Constantinople and quickly became celebrated as the most romantic way to cross the continent, spawning a host of stories and legends.

King Ferdinand I of Bulgaria (1861–1948) was passionate about speed: he would have the *Orient Express* stopped as it crossed the border, then he would climb onto the footplate and drive the train at breakneck speed down the track.

THE AMERICAS

RAILWAYS IN THE UNITED STATES

NSURPRISINGLY, THE UNITED STATES of America was among the first nations to join the railway revolution. The Baltimore and Ohio Railroad was the first to be built, in 1828. From that point on, a railway mania swept the country, helped by the fact that railways opened up the vast, untouched spaces of this expanding nation. At first, however, US railroads were heavily dependent on British technology. American engineers and industrialists spent a huge amount of effort in keeping up with the newest developments from across the Atlantic and eventually they began to develop machines that were more suited to the wide open spaces and huge distances to be covered in their country.

Early development in the US was for railroads between the major cities of the east and the rapidly developing Midwest. The city of Baltimore won that race, with a planned line out to the Ohio River, a distance of 650 km (400 miles) but although part of the line opened in 1830, it wasn't until 1853 that the river was finally reached.

Travel across the continent itself, however, remained difficult. People wishing to travel between the east and west coasts of the continent were faced with the choice of three arduous journeys. They could get a ship all the way, involving the terrifying prospect of the passage round Cape Horn; they could take their chances on an overland journey, pitting themselves against hostile Native Americans; or they could undertake the sea journey to Panama, changing there for an arduous 80-km (50-mile) trek to the Pacific through steaming jungles. And of course it wasn't just people who wished to travel; supplies and mail also had to undertake this journey. The obvious solution at the time was a railroad.

THE PANAMA RAILROAD

The settling of the Oregon Country and California provided impetus for the creation of a Panama railroad, and the California Gold Rush from 1848 created an even more urgent need. Surveying and preparation of the route began in 1849 and the terrible nature of the task soon became clear. For 13 km (8 miles), the route passed through swampy

Workers on the Panama Railroad *c.* 1910
(from the James Gordon Steese Papers, USA)

jungles filled with alligators, snakes and mosquitoes. Diseases abounded – including cholera, malaria, dysentery – and workers succumbed in their thousands. With such a high rate of attrition, labour shortages were a huge problem. Extra workers were constantly being brought in from places that included China, the West Indies, India and Ireland. Quite apart from the dangers to human life, the construction itself was a formidable challenge. Huge amounts of rock and earth had to be poured into the swamps to create a stable path for the railway to cross. Deluges of rain fell for six months in the year. A lack of construction materials in the area also meant that most necessary wood and metals had to be imported from the United States or Great Britain, driving up costs.

Money began to run out and the situation was beginning

to look extremely precarious when a stroke of good fortune occurred. Two paddle steamers filled with 1,000 passengers, mainly men looking to make their fortunes in California, were forced to seek shelter in Panama from a hurricane. The railroad across the swamp had just been completed, and while it only ran for 13 km (8 miles) as far as Gatún, it was able to transport the desperate passengers and did so charging high rates. This changed the fortunes of the company. It continued to offer the ability to travel part-way along the route and the revenues from this helped pay for the rest of its construction. Investors were also encouraged by this to put more of their money into the project.

The Panama Railroad was finally opened in 1855, after further years of toil including the construction of a huge bridge over the Chagres River (91 m or 300 ft long) and the first excavation of the Culebra Cut – later the site of a much bigger excavation project for the Panama Canal. (Ironically, of course, railroads had been supplanting canals in many countries, including the US, but Panama's famous canal was eventually to overshadow its railway.) Initially constructed at a gauge of 1,524 mm (5 ft), the same gauge used at the time in much of the southern United States, the Panama Railroad changed to standard gauge after the American Civil War.

Half a century after the opening of the Panama Railway, work started to rebuild the line on a new alignment. The construction of the Panama Canal meant that the original route would be flooded, following as it did the valley of the river Chagres. The newly aligned railway opened in 1912.

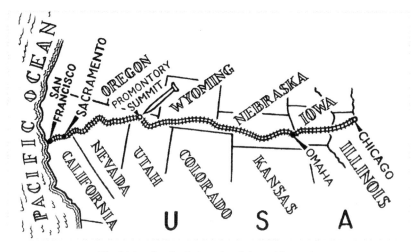

The Union Pacific Railroad and the golden spike

THE LAST SPIKE: CROSSING THE CONTINENT

Returning to the continental US, by 1860 a network was in place that connected all of the main cities of the north and Midwest. Unsurprisingly, railroad developers then turned their eyes further west, with the dream of constructing a railway from ocean to ocean. Of all the various speculators, Theodore Judah, engineer of lines as far apart as the Niagara Gorge Railroad in New York State and the Sacramento Valley Railroad in California, was the man who succeeded in persuading the powers-that-be.

Abraham Lincoln signed the Pacific Railroad Act in 1862 (in the midst of the American Civil War), authorizing a line to be built across the continent to California. Judah set about finding the optimal route, taking into account the formidable mountain barriers along the way. In addition to this small difficulty he also needed to find backers for the scheme. Luckily, at a meeting in California, he managed to persuade four local businessmen to invest. The Central Pacific Railroad Company was created with the backing of Leland Stanford (later founder of Stanford University), Charles Crocker, Mark Hopkins and Collis Huntington, collectively known as the Big Four.

Sadly for someone who had put so much effort into this project, this is where Theodore Judah leaves the story. Unhappy with the Big Four's fraudulent methods of obtaining money, he travelled back to New York with his wife to see if he could find different investors. On the way back, via Panama, he contracted yellow fever and died in New York at the age of just thirty-seven.

As might be expected of a project of this magnitude, the Central Pacific took a very long time to get going, not least because of a shortage of willing workers and of money (lost in various dishonest speculations). Finally, however, thanks to a huge influx of Chinese workers, the construction of the railway over the Donner Pass in the Sierra Nevada was completed in 1867. From this point, the route east across the plains was much easier going and at the end of the Civil War westward construction from Iowa had started,

3RD CLASS

The golden spike can still be seen at the Cantor Arts Center at Stanford University in California.
The sleeper was lost in the fires following the San Francisco earthquake in 1906.

3RD CLASS

too, under the auspices of the Union Pacific Railroad.

While the terrain itself might have been easier, construction was not, given the vast spaces to be covered and the raids of Native Americans, understandably fighting for their own territory. The hastily erected railway towns along the route of construction quickly became the stereotypes of lawlessness often associated with the Old West – drunkenness and brawls abounded.

The Central and Union Pacific Railroads finally met at Promontory Summit in Utah. On 10 May 1869, Leland Stanford and Thomas C. Durant (vice-president of the Union Pacific) took turns to drive a golden spike into a special laurel-wood sleeper (or tie in US usage). Shortly after the ceremony, for fear of theft, the golden spike and laurel sleeper were removed and replaced by standard items.

TRANS-CONTINENTAL EXPANSION

Further trans-continental railroads were constructed once the initial link had been forged. The Northern Pacific linked Minnesota and the Pacific coast, via the northern states, and the Southern Pacific ran from California to New Orleans via Arizona, New Mexico and Texas.

The very northernmost trans-continental railroad in the US was the Great Northern Railway, the brainchild of one of those geniuses of the railway age who are peppered through this story. James J. Hill was born in Ontario in 1838 and moved to St Paul, Minnesota in 1856. Trained as a bookkeeper, Hill gained valuable experience in dealing with the logistics of freight transport. He gradually built up a portfolio of businesses, buying many as they went bankrupt and selling them on at a profit once he had turned them round.

Despite its name, the St Paul and Pacific Railroad was a local concern within Minnesota and it had gone bankrupt following the global financial crisis known as the Panic of 1873. Hill researched the company and realized that there was untapped potential for development. He and his business partners raised the money to buy the company and set about expanding it, developing railroads hand in hand with industrial plants alongside them, to provide business.

By 1893, Hill's Great Northern Railway had been opened between St Paul and Seattle on the Pacific coast. He had ridden over most of the route himself, reflecting the hands-on nature of his approach to business, and had been determined that his railway would take an easier route with less need for huge engineering structures. The Great Northern was the only trans-continental route to be built without government support. Hill's control of the entire route, coupled with his flair for handling business in a depression, was a key factor in ensuring that it was one of the only routes not to face bankruptcy in the slump of the 1890s.

The final trans-continental line of the nineteenth century was the Atchison, Topeka and Santa Fe, eventually linking Chicago with Los Angeles after years of strife between competing railroad companies.

FREDERICK H. HARVEY AND THE HARVEY GIRLS

The Santa Fe was linked to another great character of railroad history, someone who brought a touch of civilization to trans-continental travel. Frederick H. Harvey was born in London in 1835 and had emigrated to the US to make his fortune. Finding work in a New York City restaurant, he rose through the ranks and gained valuable experience in all parts of the restaurant business. Following a succession of business setbacks, however, Harvey found himself working for the Chicago, Burlington and Quincy Railroad in Kansas.

MGM filmed a musical called *The Harvey Girls* in 1946, starring Judy Garland and Angela Lansbury. The film won the Oscar for Best Original Song that year with 'On the Atchison, Topeka and the Santa Fe'.

Unimpressed with the standard of catering then available on rail journeys, Harvey partnered up with the Santa Fe and began to construct restaurants along the line of the route. These became known as Harvey Houses and did a roaring trade, not least because of his policy of hiring young women to serve in the restaurants. These 'Harvey Girls' were accommodated close to their restaurants and were closely supervised and chaperoned.

As well as restaurants by the tracks, the Harvey Company also ran dining cars within the trains themselves, giving the Santa Fe an enviable reputation for excellent onboard service.

SOUTHERN STATES

Early railroad development in the southern United States followed a more problematic path than that in the north. Most railroads in the south had been constructed primarily to move cotton from plantations down to the nearest point on a river or the coast where the cargo could be loaded on to ships. These lines operated independently of one another and from the rest of the nascent network in the US, not least because the dominant gauge adopted was wider than the standard. This lack of connectivity was grievously exposed during the American Civil War. The Union implemented a programme of judicious linking of lines to allow through-running, making it much easier to move troops and materials using railroads, whereas the Confederacy had to deal with a disjointed system.

The Canadian Pacific Railway near Lake Louise, Alberta, 1927

RAILWAY DEVELOPMENT IN CANADA

Further north, the first railway in Canada was the Champlain and St Lawrence, opened in 1836 near Montreal. There followed a hiatus until the government stepped in with a system of financial inducements for construction – this in turn created a situation where railways boomed, but not always effectively. The knowledge that the government was backing a scheme whatever happened led to some hopelessly uneconomic projects, practically emptying the government coffers.

Much as in the United States, railways in Canada were used to knit the new country together. In 1871, British Columbia agreed to join the Canadian Federation with one of the conditions being that a new trans-continental route be built, linking it to the rest of the country. The British government agreed, not wanting British Columbia to fall under the aegis of the United States. (Following the purchase of Alaska from Russia, the US would then have controlled the entire Pacific coast down to the Mexican border.) The Canadian Pacific Railway was given the contract to construct the new line, contending with extremely difficult terrain over the Rockies as well as the harsh Canadian winters. In common with many other major railway projects, workers were brought in from around the world, notably from China. And in common with those other projects, working conditions were appalling, pay was dreadful and fatalities were high. Construction proceeded but costs spiralled, due to the difficulty of the terrain to be crossed. In 1885, however, the as-yet-unfinished railway proved its worth to the government, once again demonstrating that railways were the most efficient way to move large numbers of troops to where they were most needed.

The North-West Rebellion was an uprising in present-day Saskatchewan by the Métis people, in response to the perceived lack of support for their rights from the Canadian government. The Canadian Pacific demonstrated that it could move troops to quell this rebellion quickly and this provided the impetus for funds to be made available to complete the route. The full Canadian Pacific route was opened later in 1885 – at the time it was the longest railway to be constructed anywhere in the world.

The Canadian Pacific remained the only trans-continental railway in Canada until the Canadian Northern Railway completed its route from Montreal to Vancouver in 1915. Unfortunately for that company, however, the trauma of the First World War and the heavy burden of its construction costs meant that it was taken over by the Canadian government just three years later.

Incredibly, given the lack of population at the time in Canada and the extreme difficulty of building railways through the terrain, there was a third trans-continental railway, promoted by the existing Grand Trunk Railway. This was planned in two sections, centred on Winnipeg. The eastern section, to Moncton in New Brunswick on the Atlantic coast, was known as the National Transcontinental Railway. West from Winnipeg the Grand Trunk Pacific Railway was constructed through to the new city of Prince Rupert on the British Columbia coast, just south of the border with Alaska.

The NTR was planned to take a much more northerly course than that taken by the existing railways, in order to open up hitherto untapped areas of the country. It was also planned to be better engineered than the other lines, with fewer harsh gradients and curves. This clearly meant fewer concessions to the terrain and more tunnels and bridges to help keep the line as straight and level as possible. Surveying the most suitable route took years, with teams spread far and wide across the vast landscape. The crossing of the Appalachian Mountains demanded huge construction projects and the crossing of the St Lawrence River in Quebec proved to be an immense problem. The first bridge built across the river had serious design errors and collapsed in 1907, killing seventy-five workers. A second disaster happened in 1916, when the centre span of the newly designed bridge collapsed into the river while it was being hoisted into place. Thirteen workers died on that occasion. The bridge was finally completed in 1917 but through rail services on the whole NTR (the rest of which had been completed by 1913) didn't start until 1919.

THE GRAND TRUNK PACIFIC

The western part of the new route, the Grand Trunk Pacific, closely followed the route of the Canadian Northern Railway for the stretch west of Edmonton to Jasper and through the Yellowhead Pass across the Rockies. The line was completed in 1914, a few months earlier than the Canadian Northern, but the folly of building competing railway lines through such sparsely populated country became clear in 1917. It was arranged that the trains of the GTP should use those of the neighbouring CNR and the newly built tracks of the former were ripped up and sent to France as part of the war effort. Like the Canadian Northern, the Grand Trunk Pacific failed to make a profit and it was taken over by the government-owned Canadian National Railways in 1920.

Despite its early difficulties, the route of the GTP is today an integral and busy part of the Canadian national network. The port of Prince Rupert, which had long fallen behind Vancouver in terms of business, is today a major point of entry into Canada for containerized freight. Its deep natural harbour and the ability of the railway to move freight across the continent to destinations in the American Midwest means that the GTP is now carrying volumes of traffic only to be dreamed of in its early years.

CROSSING SOUTH AMERICA

There is one more trans-continental railway to describe in the Americas, although to find it we have to go a long way further south.

For the most part, the South American states came late to the railway revolution. One country that did embrace the technology and ended up with a significant network was Argentina. Prosperous and with a wide-open hinterland, lines were expanded out from the Atlantic coast, drawing in settlers and freight. Interestingly, of all of the track gauges available, Argentina plumped for 1,676 mm (5 ft 6 in), used predominantly in India and in a very few other places (although the Iberian gauge is a mere 8 mm narrower). Parts of Chile still use this gauge, as does (fairly randomly) the San Francisco Bay Area Rapid Transit System.

The arrival of the railways in Argentina, as in so many other places, created a boom. Coupled with the development of ships with refrigerated holds, Argentinian beef could be moved quickly from the interior and on to the lucrative European markets.

The Andes, however, create a formidable barrier to trade and transport the length of South America. It wasn't long before plans were set out for a railway to link Chile with Argentina and thus create a through coast-to-coast route. Unlike the efforts in Canada and the US, though, the South American route had to contend with an international border separating two frequently unstable states.

A route was surveyed, broadly following the traditional tracks taken by travellers on foot or on horseback, linking the broad-gauge railheads of Mendoza in Argentina and Santa Rosa de los Andes in Chile. Unfortunately for the future success of the line as a through route, it was decided to construct it using the metre gauge (3 ft 3½ in), meaning that any journey would need two changes of train. There were several sections of rack railway incorporated into the steepest sections of the route (see the section on mountain railways on pages 96-100).

The Transandine line was finally completed, after revolutions and financial problems, in 1910, creating a route through Valparaíso on the Pacific coast of Chile through to Buenos Aires in Argentina. Sadly, however, the railway never met its full potential. The difference in gauge played a big part – not only did passengers and freight have to transfer twice, but the narrow gauge through the mountains restricted the size of locomotives that could be used and therefore the amount of freight carried at any one time.

In 1927 the Chilean side of the railway was electrified using Swiss equipment but in 1934 a large portion of the track on the Argentinian side was swept away in a flood. This was eventually rebuilt and the line settled down to an uneventful existence for some years, but international tensions between the two countries led to the closure of the route to through traffic in the late seventies.

The Transandine closed in 1984, although governments on both sides of the Andes are now minded to support its restoration.

RAILWAYS AROUND THE REST OF THE WORLD

RAILWAY DEVELOPMENT IN RUSSIA

I N COMMON WITH SPAIN, the Russian state chose to construct its railways to a broader gauge than standard, although not to the same gauge as Spain, confusingly – Russia went with 1,524 mm (5 ft). Even more confusingly, the very first railway in Russia, built in 1837 and linking St Petersburg with the royal palaces at Tsarskoye Selo, was built to a gauge of 1,830 mm (6 ft). This proved to be a false start, however, and construction of the 1,524 mm, (later tightened to 1,520 mm) gauge line linking St Petersburg with Moscow was completed in 1851.

Russia is a country on a grand scale and in the early nineteenth century travel was extremely difficult. Roads were terrible and it could take weeks or months to travel from one city to another. Railways were the obvious solution to this problem, but, as ever, conservative and vested interests spoke out against the new technology. Luckily for railways, Tsar Nicholas I used his absolute power to push through the development of this new line.

Construction of a wider network in Russia took some time, however – not just because of the distances involved but also because the Russian economy was weak and because state authoritarianism imposed controls on who could travel.

The Trans-Siberian Railway was born out of a desire by Russia to create an effective transport link that would help defend its territory from incursion by China and by Britain via its Asian colonies and indeed via the newly constructed Canadian Pacific Railway.

Tsar Alexander III was a strong supporter of a Siberian railway and the Russian network crept ever eastwards. In 1890, the Tsarevich, later Tsar Nicholas II, inaugurated the construction from the eastern end, heading west from Vladivostok, and by the following year construction teams were heading both east and west.

TRANS-SIBERIA

The Trans-Siberian Railway opened in various stages. Until 1904 when a railway was completed around Lake Baikal, ferries were used to connect the two ends of the railway across the water. In winter, when the lake froze, a temporary railway track was run across the ice. As a railway project it was

The Trans-Siberian Railway

undoubtedly a feat of engineering, although the finished line was found to have been poorly constructed with substandard components. Not enough passing places had been built on what was predominantly a single track, so that also hindered operations. As a method for transporting troops and equipment to defend Russia from its enemies it proved hopelessly inadequate – something that the Japanese were easily able to work out when they were planning troop deployments in the Russo–Japanese War of 1904–5.

Unlike the great trans-continental railroads of North America, the Trans-Siberian didn't open up the hinterland to great swathes of settlers. The climate wasn't as suitable and in addition the differences between the political systems in the respective countries meant that the incentives and freedoms weren't in place in Russia. Today, of course, like its American counterparts, the Trans-Siberian is one of the great railway journeys of the world.

INDIA

The development of railways in India proved to be an object lesson in how to plan a network. Initially, as so often in colonial history, railways were promoted as a method of getting commodities from the interior to a port for easy transport back to the home country. In India's case this initial commodity was cotton, bound for the cloth manufacturing mills in Britain. But that aside, it was acknowledged that a vast country with a vast population would benefit from a network of lines. Unlike in Britain itself, where the railways had developed haphazardly with a multitude of different private companies building their own lines, often in competition with one another, in India a network plan was laid out with the aim of linking all of the major cities.

The prime mover for a coherent network in India was the then Governor General, Lord Dalhousie. As well as laying out the ideas for the network itself, he took the decision to specify a wider gauge than the standard, ending up with a measurement of 1,676 mm (5 ft 6 in).

As a colonial power administrating a huge territory, the British imperative in building the Indian rail network was primarily one of consolidating power: railways enabled goods and troops to be moved quickly and efficiently. The British built the railways according to their plan, irrespective of territories crossed or of the needs of the indigenous population – although local people, by and large, did end up benefiting from either increased mobility or increased economic activity. The construction itself benefited Britain enormously, with the vast majority of materials, locomotives and rolling stock all being built in Britain and exported out to India.

The first line to open was that between Bombay and Thane, on 16 April 1853. Although short (Thane today is a suburb of Mumbai) the name of the company operating the line betrayed a greater ambition – the Great Indian Peninsular Railway.

At the same time, across the other side of the country, the East Indian Railway Company was building its first line, from a location close to Calcutta, with the initial aim of reaching the coalfields of Raniganj. This line was open throughout by 1855.

Railways began to spring up across the sub-continent, though as can be imagined the terrain and climate in some areas were punishing. Mountains, forests, swamps and rivers all stood in the way of construction, but most were conquered rapidly.

RAILWAY SIGN SEEN ON AGRA STATION, INDIA, IN THE 1990s:

The time indicated on the timetable is not the time at which the train will leave; it is the time before which the train will definitely not leave.

GAUGE WARS DOWN UNDER

If India provides an example of a well-planned railway network, Australia, sadly, provides the opposite. Here there was no Lord Dalhousie to drive through a centralized and consistent plan – Australia was left with a legacy of division and delay.

The most striking and frustrating symbol of the lack of planning of the Australian network lies in the often-vexed subject of track gauge. We've seen how problems can occur if different railways are built to different gauges. In Australia, however, this lesson went astray owing to an almost farcical set of circumstances. The three most populous states in the mid-nineteenth century – Victoria, South Australia and New South Wales – determined on the Irish broad gauge of 1,600 mm (5 ft 3 in), principally at the behest of the Sydney Railway Company's chief engineer, an Irishman named F. W. Shields. Unfortunately for the future of railways in Australia, Shields resigned, to be replaced by an engineer from the British tradition who was determined to introduce the standard gauge. He was successful in pushing this through in New South Wales, but South Australia and Victoria (fairly understandably) refused to follow suit and stuck with the Irish gauge, not wishing to adapt their own systems and rolling stock. Of course, gauge doesn't really matter if you intend to have a fully enclosed system with no connection to anywhere else – logically, however, the various Australian networks did meet up (for the first time in 1883) and the problems started. To make matters worse,

Queensland, Western Australia and Tasmania had all opted for a narrower gauge – 1,067 mm (3 ft 6 in).

Since the initial chaos over rail widths, Australia has been steadily trying to sort out the situation. In 1910 the decision was taken to adopt the standard gauge throughout the country and since then efforts have been made to convert lines whenever possible.

CROSSING AUSTRALIA

One of the early beneficiaries of this policy is one of the great railway lines of the world – the Trans-Australia Railway that links Port Augusta in the east with Kalgoorlie in the west, thus creating the great trans-continental route linking Sydney with Perth. Construction started in 1912 and worked from both ends, the two work gangs meeting in 1917. This railway contains the longest stretch of dead-straight track in the world – a distance of 478 km (297 miles) – and is principally used for the transport of freight, although there are regular passenger trains along the entire route. Even this line, with standard gauge only in the middle, necessitated changes of trains at either end until the whole route was finally converted in 1970.

A striking conversion to a standard-gauge line is that of the route from Adelaide in South Australia to Alice Springs. The first part of the line was started in 1878 from Port Augusta in South Australia and was constructed to the narrow gauge of 1,067 mm (3 ft 6 in). The line didn't leave South Australia until the extension north to Alice Springs opened in 1929. The passenger train service on this line became known as the Ghan.

In 1980 a new, standard-gauge line was opened along this route, running to the west of the original line. In 2004, after many years of waiting and planning, this line was finally extended all the way up to Darwin in the Northern Territory.

CAPE TO CAIRO

Railway development in Africa became enmeshed with the expansionist policies of the imperialist Western powers of the day. The British, personified in the character of Cecil Rhodes, dreamt of one long railway threading the length of the continent, from the Cape in the south to Cairo in the north, linking the British possessions on the continent and serving as a bridgehead to further colonization. In addition, railway projects sprang up whenever significant mineral deposits were found, making the transport of the materials to ports and commercial centres much easier.

The 9,600-km (6,000-mile) total route across the continent was vastly overambitious – difficult terrain, conflicts with local people and other colonial powers plus endemic diseases, inimical wildlife and a lack of funding conspired to ensure that the project as a whole remained a dream, although some of the railways that were built endured as important pieces of infrastructure to the countries in which they sit today.

Railways in Africa quickly helped open up the continent to further expansion by the colonial powers. Towns like Salisbury in Rhodesia (now Harare in Zimbabwe) expanded rapidly once they were easy to get to and prosperity increased as goods and minerals were exchanged quickly and efficiently.

By 1898, Rhodes and his team of surveyors and labourers had managed to construct 2,200 km (1,400 miles) of railway from the Cape across the Kalahari Desert and up to Bulawayo in Southern Rhodesia. The Boer War then caused a delay to further construction, as did the death of Rhodes himself in 1902, but by 1904 the railway had reached the Victoria Falls. From there, Rhodes had planned the onward route north via the Western Rift, using ferries across the lakes encountered there, linked by sections of railway. Colonial politics, however, prevented progress. Interrupting the great swathe of British pink on the map of Africa at the time was the presence of the German colony of Tanganyika – and the Germans were not minded under any circumstances to allow the British railway to cross their territory.

But the border with Tanganyika was still some way away so the railway continued on its way north from the Falls up through Northern Rhodesia (now Zambia) and then up to and across the border with the Congo Free State. Now the Democratic Republic of Congo, this was the personal territory of King Leopold II of Belgium and was famous for being the scene of terrible atrocities against the local populations. And it was here, at a town called Bukama, that

Rhodes' vision of a Cape to Cairo railway came to an end. It was 1918, the colonial powers had exhausted themselves and even though Germany's colonies had been taken from her and distributed as spoils of war to the Allied powers, the will and impetus to continue the railway had vanished.

However, the railway that had been constructed formed the basis and core of a network that quickly emerged around it, principally to aid the extraction and export of valuable minerals.

NORTHERN AFRICA

Some time before the development of the southern part of the Cape to Cairo line, railways had been developing in the north of the continent. Indeed, the first railway in Africa had been opened in 1856 in Egypt by our old friend Robert Stephenson, linking Alexandria with Cairo. Travellers wanting to avoid the long sea journey round the Cape between Europe and Asia found this new link to be hugely useful – although it was somewhat undermined when the Suez Canal opened just a few years later. However, the railway was extended further up the Nile, reaching Luxor in 1898.

Further south lay the Sudan, scene of one of the defining moments of the British imperialist story. In 1885, General Gordon and his army had been massacred at the capital, Khartoum, by the army of the Mahdi, a local leader fighting colonial control. In order to retake the Sudan, the British authorized the construction of a military railway south from the border through to Khartoum. The route was an arduous one through burning desert, but despite the difficult terrain and local hostilities – there were skirmishes en route – construction was rapid. Started in 1896, the army with its railway arrived in the vicinity of Khartoum in 1898, where they fought the Battle of Omdurman. This led to the near-annihilation of the Mahdist forces and enabled Britain to regain control of the Sudan.

GOING UNDERGROUND

SMOKE UNDER LONDON

TRAFFIC CONGESTION IN LONDON was a major problem in the mid-nineteenth century – and the coming of the railways didn't help as they all terminated (by law) at various points just outside the main urban area. This meant that travellers had to find alternative methods of transport to get to their destinations in the centre. George Shillibeer had started his horse omnibus service in 1829 but this added to the general congestion. By mid-century, the City Fathers were looking for a more radical solution and what they came up with was an underground railway, linking Bishop's Bridge (Paddington) in the west to Farringdon, close to the main commercial centre in the east, calling at Euston, St Pancras and King's Cross main-line stations on the way. This was to

St Paul's and *The Times* offices from underground, 1875

become known as the Metropolitan Railway and would be the first underground railway in the world.

Construction of the line was hugely disruptive – there were no tunnel-boring machines at the time that could cope with such a big project so the tunnel was dug out by hand and then covered over once complete (known as the cut-and-cover method). Photographs from the period show just what this entailed and how much disruption it must have caused. The cut-and-cover method was used to construct what might be called the 'family' of Underground lines we have today, comprising the Metropolitan, District, Circle and Hammersmith & City. These lines are known as the sub-surface lines and, at the time of construction, they were run by two mutually antagonistic companies – the Metropolitan (which enjoyed the distinction of being the first underground railway company) and the District, an upstart newcomer.

The first underground trains were powered by the technology of the age – steam. As may be imagined, this created a barely tolerable atmosphere, even with regular sections running in the open air. A solution had to be found to this problem and in 1890 a newly constructed underground railway showed the way.

BORING DEVELOPMENTS

Engineers had been looking for a less disruptive method of construction than cut-and-cover. Taking inspiration from the Brunels' Shield, used to construct the Thames Tunnel, the engineer James Greathead came up with a shield that would not only allow the earth to be extracted, but also permitted concrete to be poured in while this was being done, preventing the constant collapses that had plagued the construction of that tunnel.

The first railway to be built in this fashion, and thus the first deep Tube railway in the world, was the City and South London, running from King William Street in the City of London to Elephant and Castle, a mile and half or so away

Construction of the Metropolitan District Railway, London, *c.* 1867

to the south. Most of this route, with a slight deviation to the Bank at the northern end, is now part of the Northern line. Construction started in 1886 and a year later an extension was authorized to take the line deeper into south London, to Kennington and Stockwell. Initially, the plan was to run the line using cable traction but it was soon realized that this would be impractical given the length of the new line. Steam was clearly out of the question in the narrow and enclosed tunnels so electricity was chosen as the most obvious method, even though it was then still in its infancy. The line was opened in November 1890 and thus became the world's first major electric railway.

ELECTRICITY RULES

The successful operation of electric traction on the City and South London showed the sub-surface railways the way to a brighter, cleaner future. Obviously it's less disruptive to build a new electric railway than it is to electrify an existing one, but the Metropolitan and District Railways took the decision that electrification was the only feasible option. Unfortunately, as with every other part of their relationship, they disagreed on the best method to use. The Metropolitan favoured an overhead system of wires whereas the District put its weight behind a ground-level electric rail. In the end the dispute had to go before a judge, who ruled in favour of the District, thus paving the way for the ground-level electrified system we see today. All of the District Railway was electrified by 1905, most of the Metropolitan by 1907, although electric trains didn't reach Rickmansworth until 1925. Then there was a long wait for the rest of the line – trains north of Rickmansworth to Amersham, Aylesbury and Chesham remained steam-hauled until 1961 (in which year the Metropolitan line stopped running between Amersham and Aylesbury).

The City and South London had shown the world that deep-level Tube lines were possible, and this opened the floodgates for schemes in the rest of London. These were broadly focused north of the Thames, where a thick layer of London Clay made tunnelling a lot easier than the gravels of the south. Plus, the south had already developed an extensive network of conventional railways so the need wasn't as pressing there.

MAGNUS VOLK

Earlier electric railways had been opened but only on a much smaller scale. One still operating today is Volk's Electric Railway in Brighton, constructed by Brighton-born engineer Magnus Volk and first opened in 1883. This is a narrow-gauge electric line running along the seafront between the Aquarium and a point close to Brighton Marina. Volk went on to construct one of those incredible Victorian structures that seem so utterly impractical with the benefit of hindsight.

The Brighton and Rottingdean Electric Railway was Volk's solution for a railway along the base of the cliffs – he designed a route through the surf line, consisting of two parallel railways supporting an ironwork frame with four legs, which in turn supported a platform and building for passengers. Construction started in 1894 and the railway was completed two years later. Soon after opening, however, it was nearly destroyed in a storm and extensive repairs had to be made.

The vehicle was officially known as Pioneer but it was popularly known as Daddy-Long-Legs. Described as a cross between a tram, a yacht and a seaside pier, it required a sea captain to be on board at all times and was fitted with a lifeboat and lifebuoys. It trundled up and down through the surf, proving a popular attraction

The Daddy-Long-Legs

for tourists but experiencing problems in operation. Unsurprisingly it struggled through the waves at high tide as its electric motors couldn't supply enough power, but the end came in 1900 when the local council informed Volk that they were constructing sea defences and that the railway would have to be diverted through much deeper water. This was beyond the finances of the company and operations ended in early 1901. Magnus Volk extended his electric railway along the shore as a partial replacement for the service but his brilliantly eccentric railway was lost forever.

After 1890, when the City and South London had opened, powers were granted apace for the construction of new lines. In 1892, the Great Northern and City Railway was given the go-ahead to build a Tube line from Finsbury Park to Moorgate. Interestingly, this became the only such line to be built that could accommodate full-size trains as opposed to smaller Tube-type vehicles. This line today forms part of the suburban network out to Welwyn Garden City and Hertford.

In 1893, the Charing Cross, Euston and Hampstead Railway was granted powers to build a Tube railway from Strand to Hampstead – this is most of today's Charing Cross branch of the Northern line. Also that year the Baker Street and Waterloo Railway was cleared to build between those two stations (the genesis of today's Bakerloo line).

The final years of the century saw further expansion: in 1897 the go-ahead was given for the construction of the Brompton and Piccadilly Circus Railway; in 1898 the Waterloo & City line opened between Waterloo and Bank; and in 1899 the Great Northern and Strand Railway was granted powers to build a Tube railway from Wood Green to Strand (later known as Aldwych).

This Waterloo & City line, incidentally, has always been somewhat of an anomaly. Backed by the London and South Western Railway, the line was intended to move its passengers arriving at its awkwardly located terminus at Waterloo to the City of London. It remained an anomalous line, operated by LSWR and its successors rather than London Transport right up to 1994. It remains the shortest underground line and the only one with just two stations. It is unconnected to the rest of the underground network and its vehicles have to be extracted via a crane at the Waterloo end.

Not all of the new lines were constructed as first envisioned. In 1901, the Brompton and Piccadilly Circus and the Great Northern and Strand Railways were amalgamated by a consortium owned by Charles Tyson Yerkes (see page 82). The new company, named the Great Northern, Piccadilly and Brompton Railway, incorporated a new line from Piccadilly Circus to Holborn linking the two original routes. The whole line opened on 15 December 1906, linking the District Railway at Hammersmith to the Great Northern at Finsbury

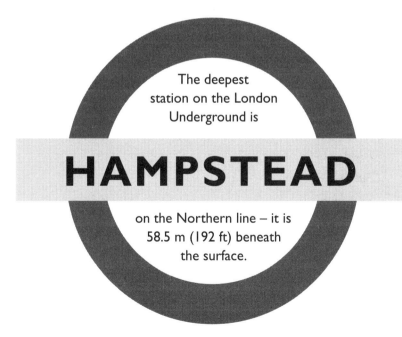

The deepest
station on the London
Underground is

HAMPSTEAD

on the Northern line – it is
58.5 m (192 ft) beneath
the surface.

Park. Today this forms the central section of the Piccadilly line. In 1907, the branch from Holborn to the Strand was opened – part of the original scheme from Finsbury Park but destined to remain a rather sorry appendix to the network now that the through line was in place.

The second deep-level Tube line to get going was the Central London Railway, running from Shepherd's Bush in the west to Liverpool Street in the east and readily identifiable as part of today's Central line.

The first escalators to be fitted at an Underground station were at Earl's Court station in 1911. William 'Bumper' Harris, a man with a wooden leg, was employed to ride up and down demonstrating their safety to any nervous passengers.

CHARLES YERKES

In the annals of railway history there are many flawed geniuses and many rogues. Genius might be too strong a word for Charles Tyson Yerkes (although rogue is probably about right) but he did have an influence on the development of the London Underground that can be seen to this day.

Born in Philadelphia in 1837, Yerkes became a banker but ended up in prison after a huge financial speculation involving public money ended in disaster and penury. On release from prison he moved to Chicago and soon became involved in the development of the mass transit system there. He put together a series of deals and ended up controlling a significant number of the city's streetcar routes, introducing electric traction on many of them to replace horses. He continued, however, to use what may be termed as shady methods to do his deals and eventually those methods caught up with him. He decided to move across the Atlantic to London to escape the increasingly torrid atmosphere he had created in Chicago.

Once in London, Yerkes partnered with Robert Perks, MP for Louth in Lincolnshire, solicitor for various railway companies and investor in underground railways. Perks suggested that Yerkes and his consortium should look at investing in the nascent Charing Cross, Euston and Hampstead Railway, which had received permission to build but had struggled to raise the money to enable it to start. Yerkes took the line on in 1900, construction began in earnest and the line opened in 1907.

Next, Yerkes took control of the District Railway (in which Perks was already a shareholder) and in 1902 he created the Underground Electric Railways Company of London (UERL), popularly known as 'The Underground' and comprising the three new deep-level Tube lines that would open in 1906–7 – the Charing Cross, Euston and Hampstead; the Baker Street and Waterloo; and the Great Northern, Piccadilly and Brompton. All of these lines were built as electric from the start – the District was electrified under the auspices of the UERL.

One of the lasting legacies of the Yerkes Tube lines was the design of the stations. The young architect Leslie Green was charged by the Underground to come up with a uniform design for the buildings. His solution was a series of steel-framed two-storey buildings, clad in ox-blood tiles and with semi-circular windows on the first floor. They had flat roofs for future development above. Green's buildings are instantly recognizable in London to this day. Sadly, though, the task of designing so many stations in such a short time (while built to a pattern, each station had to fit into the site allotted) proved too much and Leslie Green died in 1908 aged only thirty-three.

As for Yerkes, this out-and-out hustler who did so much to create the core of today's Underground network didn't even live to see the first of his new Tubes completed. He had developed kidney disease and moved back to New York, where he died in 1905.

LORD ASHFIELD AND FRANK PICK

Albert Stanley, the future Lord Ashfield, was appointed as the General Manager of the UERL in 1907, having worked in city transport authorities in the United States. Frank Pick, born in Lincolnshire and previously employed by the North Eastern Railway, had joined the UERL in 1906 as the assistant to the managing director. Soon, Stanley and Pick began the process of what would now be called brand awareness, PR and marketing that would lead to the London transport authority (under its various guises) having one of the most stylish, coherent and recognizable public images in the world. One of the earliest elements of this was the creation of the UNDERGROUND branding, featuring the famous typography with the initial and final letters larger than the others.

FINDING A SYMBOL

Photographs of Underground stations of the time show an exuberant use of the walls for advertising posters and enamel signs. This proliferation of material meant that the station name signs themselves had become more and more difficult to spot. Stanley and Pick decided to create a design of station name board that would stand out in this visual confusion and after some experimentation they settled on a blue bar showing the name against a red circle. This was the earliest manifestation of the roundel we see adorning stations, road and rail vehicles and signage today. Expanding on this, Pick determined that the system needed a common typeface to be used across all areas of activity, so he commissioned Edward Johnston, a calligrapher and typographer, to come up with one. Originally referred to as 'Underground', the font was first used in 1916 and eventually became known simply as 'Johnston'. With a few tweaks and an overhaul in the 1970s to create 'New Johnston', it is still used throughout the system today.

Hand in hand with these visual improvements, services themselves were getting better, with increased frequencies on the network leading to higher passenger numbers. Stanley was also keen on the idea of controlling services across varying transport methods and in 1912, the UERL took control of the London General Omnibus Company (known as the General), which at that time was the largest of the bus companies operating in London.

Albert Stanley became Lord Ashfield in 1920.

CHARLES HOLDEN

The next great character in the history of London's Underground was the architect Charles Holden. Known for designing the Bristol Central Library and various war memorials and cemeteries following the First World War, he had done some work for Frank Pick in the early 1920s. But in 1924 he was asked to design the run of stations for the extension of the City and South London Railway from Clapham Common down to Morden. These couldn't have been more different to the Leslie Green ox-blood tiled stations of the early century. Constructed of Portland stone, they gleamed white and proclaimed the new line with a large Underground roundel set in a glazed screen above each entrance. Three-dimensional stone roundels top pillars that appear to support a blue glass panel containing each station's name.

Holden went on to design a new, circular sub-surface ticket hall at Piccadilly Circus and the new headquarters building for the UERL at 55 Broadway, above St James's Park station. He is possibly best remembered, however, for the strikingly modern stations he created for both the eastern and western extensions of the Piccadilly Line. He and Frank Pick had toured northern Europe in 1930, gathering ideas on modern foreign architecture. Holden used this inspiration to create a collection of outstanding station buildings such as those at Sudbury Town, Arnos Grove and Southgate.

ONE COMPANY FOR ALL

By the 1920s, London's public transport system was still a mix of private companies, running tram, train, coach and bus services in varying combinations. On the roads, the General faced competition from a variety of companies known as pirate buses – these would operate over the same routes as the General, offering competitive fares, and dangerous scenes could occur at bus stops with rival vehicles jockeying into the best position to pick up the available passengers.

Pressure had been building in various quarters for one organization to oversee all transport in London in order to provide a central focus for planning, and Ramsay MacDonald's Labour government of 1929 provided the final impetus for its creation. The London Passenger Transport Board (LPTB) came into being on 1 July 1933 and was responsible for Tubes, buses, trams and trolleybuses. Main-line railways were excluded from the Act and they continued to run their own affairs. The Metropolitan Railway, which had always seen itself primarily as a main-line concern, was in fact swallowed by the new company and became the Metropolitan line.

FINDING YOUR WAY: HARRY BECK AND THE LONDON UNDERGROUND MAP

As chairman and vice-chairman of the new Board, Ashfield and Pick continued their mission to build a strong brand. One missing element was a clear and consistent map of the system. Until the early 1930s, Underground maps had been geographical, showing relative distances between stations and thus, as the system expanded, becoming too congested in the central area and too spread out in the suburbs. Harry Beck had been working as a junior draughtsman for the Underground and in his spare time he planned out a new map of the system, one not based on geography but on more even spacing and line colour-coding to convey the routes and connections more clearly. His map was initially received coolly when he presented it in 1931 – Frank Pick believing that passengers would want to see a geographically based map – but an initial print run proved successful and a regularly updated version of Beck's map has appeared on Underground stations, diaries and countless publications ever since.

TUNNELLING AND CLIMBING AROUND THE WORLD

AN UNLIKELY START

ALTHOUGH LONDON LED THE way, it was inevitable that other major cities around the world would start constructing their own underground systems. But which city had the honour of second place? If pressed, most people would probably guess Paris, New York or Berlin. In fact, the second city in the world to open an electrified underground line was ... Budapest. Built to link the centre of the city to the City Park, and running completely in the Pest side of the city, the first line of the Budapest Metro was completed in 1896. This line is now listed as a UNESCO World Heritage Site.

PARIS

As road traffic increased in density, many cities throughout the world embraced underground railways. In Paris, there had been discussions about building such a network since the mid-nineteenth century. However, protracted disagreements about the best way to achieve this meant that the first line didn't open until 1900. Running between Porte Maillot and Porte de Vincennes this forms the core of the present-day Line 1 (unsurprisingly). Once a plan was in place, however, construction proceeded rapidly, meaning that most of the first ten lines were completed by 1920.

Today the centre of Paris has a dense network of Metro stations, many of them retaining their distinctive Art Nouveau entrances, designed by Hector Guimard for the opening of the first line. Investment in underground railways in Paris, whether the Metro itself or its longer-distance cousin the RER (Express Regional Network) has been fairly constant, resulting in a rolling programme of new lines or extensions/ modernization of existing ones.

In the latter part of the twentieth century many cities around the world started to construct Metro systems, to cope with their own ever-increasing traffic problems. Today, some of these systems are the busiest in the world – notably those in Beijing, Shanghai and Seoul.

BERLIN

Traffic problems were the catalyst for subway developments across the world. In Berlin, an urban system of elevated and underground lines was constructed from the beginning of the twentieth century and developed up to the early 1930s, with a break during the First World War and during the period of financial instability that followed it.

Extensively damaged in the Second World War, re-construction proceeded quickly, along with the building of new lines. By the 1950s, the divisions between West and East Berlin were getting deeper, until the construction of the Berlin Wall in 1961 introduced the final, definitive split. Two lines that connected two parts of West Berlin via East Berlin continued to run, but the stations that now found themselves in the east were closed to all passengers. The station at Friedrichstrasse remained open to all, as it served as both an interchange and a border point.

The reunification of the city in 1989 saw the beginning of a period of renewed development, with lines reconnected and new links built.

One of the results of the London Transport connection to the design of the Moscow Metro is the layout of Gants Hill station on the Central line – it is laid out in a very similar way to stations in the Russian capital.

MOSCOW

Russia came relatively late to underground railways – the First World War, the Revolution and the ensuing civil war all conspired to push back development. With advice on construction and layout by engineers from the London Underground, the first line of the Moscow Metro opened in 1935.

Today the Moscow Metro is a large and extremely busy network, but its most noteworthy features, as far as passengers are concerned, are its stations. Built to varying architectural designs, they include some of the most flamboyantly decorated railway stations anywhere in the world.

A Moscow metro station at Novoslobodskaya

NEW YORK

Across the Atlantic, New York had built a network of elevated railways – the first one had opened in 1868 as the West Side and Yonkers Patent Railway. This later became part of the Ninth Avenue Elevated (or El). Originally operated by cables driven by stationary steam engines close to the track, the line was converted to conventional steam traction and in 1885 became the first electrified railway in New York City. It was also the first to be constructed with an extra track, meaning that some trains could run as expresses, missing out lesser-used stops and leading to the widespread and extremely useful feature of the New York Subway today. The Ninth Avenue El ran all the way from the southern tip of Manhattan up to the Bronx.

The network of elevated railways in New York City expanded so that there were tracks along Second, Third, Sixth and Ninth Avenues. However, the first underground line of the New York Subway opened in 1904 and as this network began to grow the usefulness and attraction of the Els started to wane. Subways were less subject to the extreme vagaries of the NYC climate and were also less intrusive to the people living along the line of route. The first section of elevated railway to close was the Sixth Avenue Line in 1938. The final section, the part of the Third Avenue Line that ran in the Bronx, closed in 1973. Outside Manhattan, elevated sections of the subway still exist in parts of Brooklyn, Queens and the Bronx. Parts of the railway infrastructure on Staten Island, although not officially part of the subway, are also elevated.

Curve at Brooklyn Terminal, Brooklyn Bridge, New York, 1898

CHICAGO

Elsewhere in the US, Chicago retains its elevated railway. The first 'L', as it is known, opened in 1892, but the early network suffered from the fact that elevated railways were not permitted downtown unless permission was granted by all of the property owners along the line of route. This is where the familiar name of Charles Yerkes comes into the story once again. Already controlling most of the city's streetcars, Yerkes used all of the dirty methods at his disposal to get over the obstacles. Despite its shady provenance, the resulting lines through downtown Chicago created a network that is still in use today.

THE FIRST ELEVATED LINE

Elevated lines are almost as old as railways themselves – the first such line was the London and Greenwich, opened between London Bridge and Greenwich from 1836 to 1838. Built entirely on a brick viaduct, this was the first passenger railway in the capital and today it forms part of the extremely busy network of routes running into south-east London. Greenwich was the terminus of the line up until 1878. From there it was extended in a tunnel under what is now the National Maritime Museum and out to Charlton, linking with the existing railway there.

CLIMB EVERY MOUNTAIN

Until now we have looked at what are referred to as adhesion railways, often constructed in the early days of steam when engineers did what they could to keep lines as level as possible. An adhesion railway is one that runs without the aid of additional devices such as ropes or cogs and relies only on the friction between the steel rail and wheel. Not only was it important to keep things level to avoid trains stalling going up steep banks or running away when coming down, but steam locomotive boilers also needed to be kept as level as possible so that key internal components such as the boiler Tubes were kept covered in water at all times. Clearly, keeping on the level wasn't going to be possible everywhere – tunnelling and bridging, digging cuttings and building embankments are costly processes and not everywhere was suitable anyway. One famous example of a steep slope on the British railway network, in use today, is the Lickey Incline between Bromsgrove and Barnt Green in Worcestershire, on the main line between Bristol and Birmingham (completed in 1841). Here the railway needs to surmount the Lickey Ridge and to do this it was engineered up a two-mile bank with a gradient of 2.65 per cent. This was a fearsome task for the engines of the day and a system of banking engines was introduced (a banking engine is one that pushes a train from the back, giving extra power to help the locomotive at the front). Even today, with modern diesel traction, there are banking engines ready to assist heavy freights up the bank.

The Lickey Incline, however, is by no means the steepest

adhesion-worked railway. The gradient of the Hopton Incline on the Cromford and High Peak Railway in Derbyshire was 7.1 per cent, though it was not directly comparable as it was on a mineral line and therefore didn't see the heavy freight and expresses services of the Lickey. Still steeper adhesion railways can be found elsewhere in the world – there is a part of the Lisbon tramway system at 14.5 per cent, for example – but it is clear that adhesion railways find sustained inclines hard work.

As a result, mountainous countries or regions needed to find a way of getting railways to work up and down gradients in a safer and more effective way. One of the earliest principles was a funicular system using ropes and counterbalances to haul loads up and take them down steep slopes. Extraordinarily, one of these early systems is still in use today – it can be found in Salzburg, Austria, and is called the Reisszug. First mentioned as early in 1515, a single car takes goods up from the city and into the Hohensalzburg Castle. Modern funicular railways generally involve a steel cable attached to a pair of vehicles on adjoining tracks. Each vehicle counterbalances the other as they travel up and down.

RACK AND PINION

In the very early days of steam locomotives, the engineers of the Middleton Railway (a coal railway in Leeds, Yorkshire) feared that any locomotive they got to run on their lines

Festungsbahn funicular railway, Austria

would have to be light enough not to break their rails – which were formed of cast iron and therefore more brittle than the later steel – but would therefore not be strong enough to get the grip needed to pull the loaded coal wagons. The solution developed in 1811 by the colliery manager, John Blenkinsop, was to relay the track with a toothed rail (a rack) on one side and then to commission a locomotive with a pinion (or gear) that could mesh with it and aid traction.

As railway technology developed, it was soon found that rack-and-pinion systems were not needed on most conventional railways. For mountain tracks, however, they would be a great solution.

The first mountain rack railway in the world was opened in 1868 in the US – the Mount Washington Cog Railway in New Hampshire – using a system developed by Sylvester Marsh. At the same time, over in Switzerland, Niklaus Riggenbach was developing his own rack-and-pinion system and this was adopted for the new Vitznau-Rigi Bahn, opened in 1871. Both of these railways still exist today.

Many early rack railways were operated by steam, so despite the incline the steam locomotive boilers still needed to stay as level as possible. The solution adopted by many railways was to construct locomotives with tilted boilers, so that on the crucial mountain sections the boiler would always be level. This of course had the consequence that they couldn't operate for long on level sections – the fact that many mountain railways were early adopters of electric traction was partly to remove the need for such inflexible arrangements.

Rack railways generally have low overall speeds so for standard railways passing through mountainous regions other solutions have to be adopted. Switzerland has constructed miles of tunnels through its mountains to carry trains across its territory. Between Frutigen and Kandersteg, in order to climb out of the Kander valley, the Bern–Lötschberg–Simplon line heading south turns sharply north in a tunnel then after some distance enters another tunnel in which it changes direction to south once more. Anyone standing in the valley can see the same train passing three times at different levels as the track climbs.

Today some mountain railways have been officially recognized as sites of international importance, thanks to their outstanding engineering and the landscapes through which they pass. Three of the remaining mountain railways in India have been given World Heritage Site status by UNESCO; collectively known as the 'Mountain Railways of India', these are the Darjeeling Himalayan Railway, the Nilgiri Mountain Railway and the Kalka Shimla Railway.

Other World Heritage Sites include the Rhaetian Railway, which links Switzerland and Italy via two Alpine passes, and the Semmering Railway in Austria, which was built over 41 km (25 miles) of high mountains in the mid-nineteenth century.

THE NEED FOR SPEED

FRENCH BEGINNINGS

WE HAVE SEEN HOW railway companies in many countries worked tirelessly to increase speeds on their most important routes. All of this took place on standard lines but it quickly became clear that if a leap in speeds were to occur then special infrastructure would have to be built.

But what do we mean by high-speed rail? How fast is fast? There isn't an internationally recognized definition of high speed – different countries adopt different measures. The European Union defines high-speed rail as having infrastructure that has been either built specially or has been upgraded for high-speed trains. Minimum speeds apply: 250 km/h (155 mph) on lines specially built for high speed and 200 km/h (124 mph) on existing upgraded lines. The trains themselves must have been designed to be fully compatible with the infrastructure to ensure complete safety and that service standards are met.

After the Second World War, the French national railway company, the SNCF, led the world in high-speed rail development. By 1954, one of their locomotives had hauled a train at 243 km/h (150 mph) on a test run. The following year, these test speeds had increased to 331 km/h (206 mph). As a guide to how revolutionary this was, today's Eurostar train between London and Paris/Brussels runs at a top speed of 300 km/h (186 mph).

While the French were conducting these successful experiments, a country on the other side of the world was starting its own high-speed rail programme, one that would change the face of rail travel for ever.

JAPAN

Japan in the 1950s was a bruised and battered country after the trauma of the Second World War. Lacking natural oil and gas resources, around half of Japan's electricity output was achieved using coal, of which it did have its own supply. Reluctant to import vast amounts of petroleum, the Japanese government turned to railways as the most effective way to move its population around the country. By 1957, taking inspiration and ideas from the work being done in France,

Japanese engineers had constructed the first high-speed line in Tokyo, using the then widespread Japanese narrow gauge of 1,067 mm (3 ft 6 in). The decision was then taken to adopt standard gauge for future lines, in order to create greater stability at the speeds being sought.

Construction began on the first new Inter-City high-speed line between Tokyo and Osaka in 1959 and test runs on the new structure reached 256 km/h (159 mph) just four years later. The line opened to the public in 1964, in time to transport the vast numbers of people attending the Tokyo Olympic Games. The new service was named *Shinkansen*, meaning 'new main line'.

Since then, Japan has expanded its network dramatically and has become renowned for operating a system that is clean, fast and efficient, with punctuality standards of which other countries can only dream.

Japan clearly led the field in adopting high-speed rail technology for normal service, but it has been taken up enthusiastically by railway companies around the world, principally in Europe, where the tradition of rail travel is strong, but increasingly elsewhere, most notably in China.

BRITAIN

The story of high-speed rail in Britain is a frustrating one, involving missed opportunities and a long wait for the construction of the first truly high-speed line.

In the 1960s, thought was given to developing a new generation of trains for Britain's railways, involving technology to enhance speeds on existing lines, such as improved track profiling and tilting mechanisms onboard trains. Delays to the project meant that by the early seventies authorization was given for the development of a new generation of diesel trains, designed to work on existing tracks but at speeds of up to 200 km/h (125 mph).

The first production locomotives began to be delivered in 1975 and, together with a new design of passenger coach, they entered service the following year on the Western Region routes out of London Paddington to destinations in the west of England and south Wales. The trains, known as InterCity 125s or High Speed Trains (HSTs), revolutionized services and began to attract people back to rail travel in Britain. Soon they began to appear on the East Coast main-line services to the north east of England and eastern Scotland, as well as on the Cross Country routes centred on Birmingham. An HST in 1987 broke the world speed record for a diesel-powered train, topping out at 238 km/h (148 mph).

It's a testament to the design of both these locomotives and the coaching stock that at the time of writing (2015) they remain in full revenue-earning service with no sign of withdrawal.

While the HSTs were being designed and manufactured, British Rail continued to research and develop technology for tilting trains. These could be used to increase speeds along existing lines, without the need for new, dedicated lines. The new Advanced Passenger Train was unveiled to the public in

1981. Unfortunately, as might be expected from any brand-new equipment, problems occurred with the tilt mechanism, most disastrously from a public relations point of view on a press run. Passengers complained of travel sickness as the coaches leaned into the curves and the resultant press coverage led to a loss of nerve at the political level. The project was dropped, despite the huge sums already spent and despite indications that the trains were beginning to perform as they should. The patents for the tilting mechanisms were sold to the Italian company Fiat Ferroviaria, which developed them into their own trains, known as *Pendolinos* (from the Italian for pendulum). Pendolino technology was incorporated into new trains for several different national rail networks including, frustratingly for the original developers, the West Coast main line in the UK – the line for which the original APT had been designed. A further frustration for British railway operators (and passengers) is that while the West Coast Pendolinos were designed for a top speed of 225 km/h (140 mph), they can only run at a maximum of 200 km/h (125 mph) because of the constraints of the current signalling system. It remains a possibility that further work can be done to upgrade systems to allow for faster running.

The only high-speed railway line currently in operation in Britain (HS1) is the line that links London to Paris and Brussels, passing through the Channel Tunnel between Britain and France. The government is currently pushing ahead with its plans for a second high-speed line (HS2), which is planned to run from London up through Birmingham then splitting to serve Manchester and Leeds.

EUROPE

The French railway company (SNCF) continued to invest in development of its own high-speed rail programme through the sixties and seventies, culminating in the opening of the first high-speed line (LGV or *ligne à grande vitesse*) between Paris and Lyon in 1981. Since then, there has been a progressive opening of further high-speed lines throughout the country, including the line north from Paris that carries the cross-Channel Eurostar services. Whereas the French high-speed rail strategy consisted of building new, long stretches of line to connect centres of population via relatively sparsely populated countryside, Germany adopted a different approach. It did build new stretches of line but its high-speed services run over more of the original rail network, reflecting the fact that population centres are more closely packed than they are in France.

The first German high-speed service started in 1991 and ran across the country from Hamburg in the north to Munich in the south.

Today, reflecting the interconnection of much of Europe's high-speed network, trains run across international borders to cities in Austria, Belgium, France, the Netherlands and Switzerland. To enable this, trains were introduced carrying multiple electrical packages to take into account the fact that different countries electrified their railways with different systems and at different voltages.

Italy came early to the concept of new high-speed lines, opening the *Direttissima* line between Rome and Florence in 1977, four years before the first line opened in France. Development was slower than in the latter country, however, but today there are high-speed services operating from Turin and Milan in the north down to Salerno in the south, with services projecting further to Bari and down towards Sicily.

Spain has adopted high-speed rail with gusto, no doubt due to the fact it is a country with widely spread centres of population. The first new line was opened in 1992 and, as with the Japanese *Shinkansen*, this was built to standard gauge and therefore had no physical links to the existing network. Development proceeded apace and today Spain's high-speed network is the second largest in the world (after another precocious late developer – China) and connects at the French border with the rest of the European network.

So important is high-speed rail to Europe that the European Union has in place the Trans-European High-Speed Rail Network directive, which ensures interoperability between national networks to create integrated routes across the continent. Several major corridors have been identified, including the routes from Berlin down to Palermo; the high-speed lines radiating from Brussels to London, Paris, Amsterdam and Cologne; the lines in the Iberian peninsula and up into south-west France and the route between Paris and Bratislava.

CHINA

The story of recent railway development in China is an astonishing one. Early development was slow and stuttering. As elsewhere in the world it was Western powers (notably Britain) that led the way in constructing railways, keen to exploit the natural resources available in China. Unlike India, however, Western power in China was restricted to enclaves and trade missions and the Chinese government was deeply suspicious of and hostile to the new technology. It wasn't only the government that was hostile – in a country with a huge population, many workers deeply feared (not unreasonably and certainly not uniquely) that the new technology would help to throw them out of work. It was only in 1895 that the government permitted foreign interest to develop railways in the country and it wasn't until 1909 that the first all-Chinese-backed line was opened.

Railway development in the first half of the twentieth century was slow, with conflicts restricting the local ability to expand, although the invading Japanese did put a programme of railway construction in place in Manchuria. In the second half of the century, however, thanks to heavy investment by the People's Republic, the Chinese network developed rapidly. Technologically, though, it remained firmly in the steam age – limitless coal and labour meant that initially the impetus to adopt other technologies wasn't there. New steam locomotives continued to be produced up to 1999, but the end for steam then came very quickly, with the current emphasis on building modern, electrically powered high-speed lines.

An astonishingly fast-paced programme of line building has meant that China is now the home of the world's largest network of high-speed railway lines – 19,000 km (12,000 miles) – including the longest high-speed line in the world linking Beijing and Hong Kong. In 2015, the Chinese government announced plans for a high-speed line to be built between Beijing and Moscow, in conjunction with Russia. This would be an astonishing achievement – a spend of $242bn for a line 7,000 km (4,350 miles) in length, planned to slash journey times between the cities to two days. This also raises the theoretical possibility of a through high-speed train from London to Beijing!

Not content with this, China also boasts the fastest regular train service anywhere, albeit not on a conventional railway system. The Shanghai Maglev Train operates between Shanghai Pudong International Airport and Pudong itself – a distance of 30 km (18.5 miles). 'Maglev' is an abbreviation of 'magnetic levitation' – trains are levitated and propelled along a central guide-way by powerful magnets. The system allows for extremely high speeds – the Shanghai Maglev Train reaches a top speed in everyday service of 431 km/h (268 mph).

On 21 April 2015, an experimental Maglev train owned by the Central Japan Railway broke the world speed record, reaching 603 km/h (374 mph)

UNITED STATES: STREAMLINED FOR SPEED

Up until the 1950s, passenger numbers on America's railroad network remained high, with trains for the most part being the quickest and most convenient way to travel long distances. From the 1930s, the railroad companies caught the buzz of the age – streamlining. Strikingly streamlined steam locomotives were introduced, as well as lightweight streamlined diesel trains.

In 1934, the Union Pacific Railroad introduced its M-10000 streamlined passenger train, using petroleum distillate as fuel. With its three articulated cars it was a strikingly different-looking train for its time and place. Painted in the then-new bright yellow shade known as 'Armour Yellow', it drew huge crowds on its initial tours of the network. But it was its successor that really made the headlines – the M-10001. This was a diesel-electric unit made up of six articulated cars and built in a similar striking design to its earlier cousin. Incorporating sleeping cars and an observation car it was introduced in October 1934 – and that same month it completed a record-breaking crossing of the continent, running from Los Angeles to New York in fifty-seven hours, a hugely impressive fourteen hours faster than the previous record. Following this triumph, M-10001 was placed in regular service on the Chicago to Portland, Oregon route, taking forty hours as opposed to the previous fastest time of fifty-eight hours.

Elsewhere, the Chicago, Burlington and Quincy Railroad introduced its Zephyr diesels in 1934. On 26 May that year, the *Pioneer Zephyr* travelled the 1,600 km (1,000 miles) between Denver and Chicago in a record-breaking time of thirteen hours, reaching a top speed of 181 km/h (112.5 mph). In addition to this, the lightweight construction of the trains enabling fuel efficiency meant that they were soon a hit with passengers and operators alike. Zephyrs went on to work a network of services across the Midwest and down to Texas.

In 1937 the Atchison, Topeka and Santa Fe introduced its Super Chief service on its own route between Los Angeles and Chicago. This was an all-Pullman sleeping-car train with high standards of service that soon became known as 'The Train of the Stars', transporting as it did many of the actors of the day to and from Hollywood. Diesel-hauled, the Super Chief not only reduced the overall time for the journey, bringing it down to forty hours, but it was uniquely operated all the way by the same company, enabling a consistently high standard of service to be implemented for the whole journey.

The End of the Heyday

The 1930s, 1940s and early 1950s were a heyday for long-distance passenger railways in the United States, with big, bold trains crossing the continent and strong public relations departments creating striking advertising images that have the power to stir the blood even today. A parallel exists, however, with the situation in Britain at around the same time (notwithstanding the much higher cost the Second World War exacted on the British railway infrastructure). Both countries were developing high-speed, luxurious headline services with the full force of their marketing teams behind them. Behind this, however, the Great Depression led to the withdrawal of services on both sides of the Atlantic. In the US, automobiles began to eat away at rail passenger numbers, as did the burgeoning network of road coach companies, most notably Greyhound, which by the mid-1930s was already carrying more passengers than the main railroads.

The years following World War Two saw developments in both automotive technology and the construction of an ever-expanding network of highways and freeways. Large volumes of freight left the railroads to be transported by truck and passengers continued to drift away from both railroads and coach operators as automobiles became more reliable and more luxurious. The arrival of the commercial airliner saw most of the long-distance demand transfer to air travel.

Although large volumes of freight were still being carried, by the late 1960s outside of some of the big cities passenger rail services in the US were in big trouble, with several companies filing for insolvency. The situation came to a head in 1970 when the Nixon administration created the National Railroad Passenger Corporation, an organization that would use public money to help support passenger rail services. Operated under the brand name of *Amtrak*, it started operations in 1971 and continues to run many services today, although many of them are away from the big centres of population at very limited frequencies and at relatively low speeds. One major obstacle currently in the way of higher speeds across much of the US rail network is a widely applied speed limit of 127 km/h (79 mph), put in place after a severe crash in Illinois in 1946. This limit applies to trains that are not fitted with some form of automatic train protection/automatic

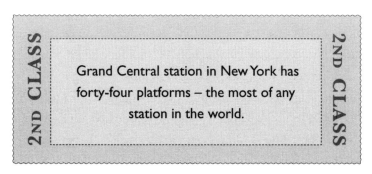

2ND CLASS

Grand Central station in New York has forty-four platforms – the most of any station in the world.

2ND CLASS

braking systems. Widespread implementation of such systems has not been put in place, resulting in a relatively slow-speed network.

High-Speed Revival

Rail technology is certainly not moribund in the US, however. Despite the historic decline in passenger services, there have been developments in the field of American high-speed lines. In 1969, a *Metroliner* service was introduced between Washington DC and New York City via Baltimore and Philadelphia, running at speeds of up to 200 km/h (125 mph). This ran until 2006, when it was replaced by the *Acela* high-speed service running on an extended network up to Boston, Massachusetts. Using tilting technology, the Acela trains are currently the fastest in the Americas and can reach speeds of 240 km/h (150 mph). These high speeds are restricted, however, by the fact that the trains do not have their own track and have to share the existing ageing infrastructure with slower services.

There are plans to develop a high-speed line along this rail route, known as the Northeast Corridor, in order to bring down transit times between the major cities that are located along it. Current aspirations are for it to be in place by 2040.

In recent years, too, plans for high-speed services in various different states have been put forward, most notably the California High-Speed Rail project. The proposal for a high-speed line to link Los Angeles with San Francisco – with trains travelling at up to 320 km/h (200 mph) – was put to the public vote in 2008, with 52.62 per cent of voters approving the project. Construction started in January 2015, with a projected start of service in 2029. Further extensions to the route are planned to San Diego and Sacramento.

Major cities in the US still rely on (or have come to rely on) extensive suburban rail, rapid transit and/or subway systems. New York's is the biggest but other cities are continuing to develop their systems; Chicago, Boston and Philadelphia all have long-established rapid transit networks, while Washington DC's Metro, only opened in 1976, has become the country's second-busiest system in terms of passenger numbers, after New York City. Even a city as famously reliant on cars as Los Angeles has a network, the first line of which opened in 1990.

ART AND CULTURE

RAILWAYS IN LITERATURE

R AILWAYS TODAY, ELECTRIFICATION AND high speed not-withstanding, tend to represent stability and tradition. An arched viaduct striding across a country valley adds a settled view to the scene and it's easy to forget that railways were once seen as revolutionary technology, carving up the countryside and enabling people to travel at seemingly incredible speeds. Before the coming of railways, no one had travelled faster than the speed of a galloping horse. All sorts of fears were raised that rail travellers would be suffocated as the air was forced from their lungs at terrifying speeds. Unsurprisingly, the new possibilities opened up by rail travel served as a rich source of inspiration for many writers from the nineteenth century onwards.

Charles Dickens

One of the finest expressions of this early attitude to railways comes in *Dombey and Son*, Charles Dickens' 1848 novel of overweening pride, money and familial dysfunction. Dickens had seen the huge disruption caused by the construction of the London to Birmingham railway where it crashed through the existing settlement of Camden in north London on its way to the Euston terminus. Even today it's easy to imagine just how disruptive this was, when you consider the width and depth of the existing cutting. In *Dombey and Son*, Camden becomes 'Stagg's Garden' and this passage sums up the despair felt by many at this new, terrifying force:

The first shock of a great earthquake had, just at that period, rent the whole neighbourhood to its centre. Traces of its course were visible on every side. Houses were knocked down; streets broken through and stopped; deep pits and trenches dug in the ground; enormous heaps of earth and clay thrown up; buildings that were undermined and shaking, propped by great beams of wood. Here, a chaos of carts, overthrown and jumbled together, lay topsy-turvy at the bottom of a steep unnatural hill; there, confused treasures of iron soaked and rusted in something that had accidentally become a pond. Everywhere were bridges that led nowhere; thoroughfares that were wholly impassable; Babel towers of chimneys, wanting half their height; temporary wooden houses and enclosures, in the most unlikely situations; carcases of ragged tenements, and fragments of unfinished walls and arches, and piles of scaffolding, and wildernesses of bricks, and giant forms of cranes, and tripods straddling above nothing. There were a hundred thousand shapes and substances of incompleteness, wildly mingled out of their places, upside down, burrowing in the earth, aspiring in the air, mouldering in the water, and unintelligible as any dream. Hot springs and fiery eruptions, the usual attendants upon earthquakes, lent their contributions of confusion to the scene. Boiling water hissed and heaved within dilapidated walls; whence, also, the glare and roar of flames came issuing forth; and mounds of ashes blocked up rights of way, and wholly changed the law and custom of the neighbourhood.

In short, the yet unfinished and unopened Railroad was in progress; and, from the very core of all this dire disorder, trailed smoothly away, upon its mighty course of civilization and improvement.

Dickens became an enthusiastic railway user as the network expanded across Britain – and indeed his travels around North America were also facilitated by the burgeoning network there. Here is a disquieting extract from the chapter 'An American Railroad' in his book *American Notes*, written following his visit there in 1842:

There are no first- and second-class carriages as there are with us, but there is a gentlemen's and a ladies' car: the main distinction between which is that in the first, everybody smokes, and in the second, nobody does. As a black man never travels with a white one, there is also a negro car; which is a great, blundering, clumsy chest, such as Gulliver put to sea in, from the kingdom of Brobdingnag. There is a great deal of jolting, a great deal of noise, a great deal of wall, not much window, a locomotive engine, a shriek and a bell.

However, on 9 June 1865, Dickens had an experience that was to change his view completely and which, some say, led to his life ending prematurely. He was on the way back from France with his mistress Ellen Ternan and her mother. The Folkestone to London boat train, operated by the South Eastern Railway, derailed while crossing a viaduct at Staplehurst, Kent. Some workmen had removed a section of track because they had misread the timetable and had thought no train was due. The incident was exacerbated by the fact that the look-out man, who should have been positioned 1,000 yards down the line with a red flag in case of approaching trains, had been just under half that distance away. This meant that the train, travelling at 72–80 km/h (45–50 mph), didn't have enough time to react to the flag before hitting the section of trackless railway and crashing off the viaduct and into the River Beult. The carriage in which Dickens was travelling was left hanging over the bridge. Dickens managed to climb out of the carriage and help his companions to safety. He then went down to the river, where the unluckier carriages and passengers were lying smashed and broken, and dispensed water, brandy and kind words to the survivors, some of whom were clearly dying. Once he had done what he could, he suddenly remembered that the early manuscript of *Our Mutual Friend* was still in the carriage. Remarkably, he climbed back into the wreckage to retrieve it. Once back in London the shock overtook him and he continued to have disturbing flashbacks for the rest of his life.

One of Dickens' most memorable short stories, 'The

Signalman', appeared the year after this crash. An eerie story, it tells the tale of a haunted signalman who has twice seen a mysterious, waving figure just before a tragedy strikes. He tells of how the apparition has recently reappeared and how he fears that tragedy will strike anew.

Leo Tolstoy

Tolstoy viewed railways as a disorientating modern invention, sweeping away his familiar world. In *Anna Karenina* (1877), Levin's attitude towards railways mirrors Tolstoy's own:

> *Next morning Constantine Levin left Moscow and toward evening he reached home. On the way back in the train he talked with his fellow-passengers about politics and the new railways, and felt oppressed, just as in Moscow, by the confusion of the views expressed, by discontent with himself and a vague sense of shame. But when he got out of his train at his station and by the dim light from the station windows, saw his one-eyed coachman, Ignat, with his coat-collar turned up, and his sledge with its carpet-lined back, his horses with their tied-up tails, and the harness with its rings and tassels, and while Ignat, while still putting the luggage into the sledge, began telling him the village news: how the contractor had come, and Pava had calved, – Levin felt that the confusion was beginning to clear away and his shame and self-dissatisfaction to pass.*

Émile Zola

In France, possibly the finest evocation of railways in literature is Émile Zola's *La Bête humaine* (1890). This is the murder scene:

First Jacques saw the mouth of the tunnel light up, like the door of a furnace full of blazing wood. Then, bringing the din with it, the engine poured forth with its dazzling round eye, its headlamp blazing a gap through the landscape and lighting the rails far ahead with a double line of flame. But that was but a flash – the whole line of carriages followed, the little square windows, blindingly light, making a procession of crowded compartments tear by at such a dizzying speed that the eye was not sure whether it had really caught the fleeting visions. And in that precise quarter-second Jacques quite distinctly saw through the window of a brilliantly lit coupe a man holding another man down on the seat and plunging a knife into his throat, while a dark mass, probably a third person, possibly some luggage that had fallen from above, weighed down hard on the kicking legs of the man being murdered. Already the train had gone and was disappearing towards La Croix-de-Maufras, showing no more of itself in the darkness than the three red lamps, the red triangle.

Agatha Christie and Other Thriller Writers

Agatha Christie is seen as the pre-eminent British crime writer of the twentieth century and three of her most popular titles involve railways as the central element – *The Mystery of the Blue Train* (1928), *Murder on the Orient Express* (1934), and *4.50 from Paddington* (1957). The first two titles had the additional romance of being set on continental overnight expresses. As was *Stamboul Train* by Graham Greene (1932) – like *Murder on the Orient Express* it is set on the Istanbul express, albeit travelling in the opposite direction. Other thrillers associated with railways include Patricia Highsmith's *Strangers on a Train* (1950); *The Taking of Pelham One Two Three* by John Godey (1973); *Avalanche Express* by Colin Forbes (1978) and the Jim Stringer railway detective novels by Andrew Martin.

TRAINS ON FILM

Film producers have long seen the potential of movies set on or around railways. Most of the titles mentioned above have been adapted for film or television and one of the very earliest motion pictures was the Lumière Brothers' *Train Pulling into a Station* (1895). Here is just a small selection of films in which trains and railways are central to the plot: *Oh Mr Porter* (1937) stars Will Hay as a hapless railway worker sent to a remote station in Ireland; *The Lady Vanishes* (1938) is a relatively early Alfred Hitchcock film set on a train as it travels through Europe; Noel Coward's evocative *Brief Encounter* (1945) was filmed at Carnforth station in Lancashire and has the railway as the unifying location; *The Titfield Thunderbolt* (1953) is a hilarious pre-Beeching paean to rural railways and the threat posed by road transport; *The Great St Trinian's Train Robbery* (1966) takes the chaos of St Trinian's and applies it to the rigid form and structure of railways.

RAILWAYS IN ART

In the nineteenth century, unsurprisingly, railways become a fitting subject for paintings. In 1844, J.M.W. Turner had exhibited *Rain, Steam and Speed – The Great Western Railway*, depicting a train crossing Brunel's Maidenhead railway bridge. William Powell Frith, one of the greatest artists of Victorian scenes, had had enormous success with his monumental depiction of a human crowd in *The Derby Day* (1858). It was only a matter of time before he turned his gaze to the hustle and bustle of the ever-expanding railways and in 1862 he produced *The Railway Station*, a view of the chaos reigning at London's Paddington Station and depicting nearly a hundred separate individuals.

In France, the Impressionists had realized the rich pickings enabled by the smoky, steamy atmosphere associated with the railways. Pissarro's *Lordship Lane, Dulwich* (1871), depicts a train on the (now defunct) Crystal Palace branch in what was then a fairly rural setting. He also painted *The Railway Bridge at Pontoise* (1873) and *The Train, Bedford Park* (1897). Monet created *The Railway Station at Argenteuil* in 1871 and the *Gare St Lazare* in 1877, while Van Gogh gave us *Landscape with Carriage and Train in the Background* (1890).

In the twentieth and twenty-first centuries, photography and film became the dominant art forms for capturing railway scenes, although some significant railway artists produced and continue to produce work. One of the greatest was Terence Cuneo (1907–96) – an artist best known today for his railway paintings but who had a huge body of work including military and ceremonial scenes (he was designated the official painter at the Coronation of HM Elizabeth II). Because of the length of his career, Cuneo has left us scenes depicting the railways as they were in the 1940s and 1950s right up to a painting of the Eurotunnel Le Shuttle in the Channel Tunnel.

Cuneo was one of the Fellows of the Guild of Railway Artists. There have only been five such Fellows at the time of writing – the others are John Austin, Philip Hawkins, Malcolm Root and David Shepherd.

Landscape with Carriage and Train in the Background,
by Vincent Van Gogh, 1890

RAILWAYS IN POETRY

By the early twentieth century the railway had become a familiar part of daily life, no longer the thrusting new technology it had been in the past eighty to ninety years. Yet it continued to inspire poets in numerous different ways, as the following examples show.

Thomas Hardy

In his poem, 'Midnight on the Great Western', Hardy muses on a young boy sitting listlessly and seemingly without interest on a train – how can he be so uncaring about the journey he is on? Obviously the train here represents life's journey itself.

In the third-class seat sat the journeying boy,
And the roof-lamp's oily flame
Played down on his listless form and face,
Bewrapt past knowing to what he was going,
Or whence he came.

In the band of his hat the journeying boy
Had a ticket stuck; and a string
Around his neck bore the key of his box,
That twinkled gleams of the lamp's sad beams
Like a living thing.

What past can be yours, O journeying boy
Towards a world unknown,
Who calmly, as if incurious quite

On all at stake, can undertake
This plunge alone?

Knows your soul a sphere, O journeying boy,
Our rude realms far above,
Whence with spacious vision you mark and mete
This region of sin that you find you in,
But are not of?

The idea of a railway journey as a metaphor for life occurs again in 'Faintheart in a Railway Train':

At nine in the morning there passed a church,
At ten there passed me by the sea,
At twelve a town of smoke and smirch,
At two a forest of oak and birch,
        And then, on a platform, she:

A radiant stranger, who saw not me.
I said, 'Get out to her, do I dare?'
But I kept my seat in my search for a plea,
And the wheels moved on. O could it but be
        That I had alighted there!

Edward Thomas

In Edward Thomas's poem 'Adlestrop', published in 1917 and referring to a journey he had taken in 1914 between Oxford and Worcester, the train is an integral part of the landscape – the sound of the train is just another part of the soundscape:

Yes, I remember Adlestrop –
The name, because one afternoon
Of heat the express-train drew up there
Unwontedly. It was late June.

The steam hissed. Someone cleared his throat.
No one left and no one came
On the bare platform. What I saw
Was Adlestrop – only the name

And willows, willow-herb, and grass,
And meadowsweet, and haycocks dry,
No whit less still and lonely fair
Than the high cloudlets in the sky.

And for that minute a blackbird sang
Close by, and round him, mistier,
Farther and farther, all the birds
Of Oxfordshire and Gloucestershire.

Wilfred Owen

In contrast to the peaceful scene described in the previous poem, in 'The Send-Off' (1918), Wilfred Owen describes the departure of a train carrying troops to the trenches of the First World War.

Down the close, darkening lanes they sang their way
To the siding-shed,
And lined the train with faces grimly gay.

Their breasts were stuck all white with wreath and spray
As men's are, dead.

Dull porters watched them, and a casual tramp
Stood staring hard,
Sorry to miss them from the upland camp.
Then, unmoved, signals nodded, and a lamp
Winked to the guard.

So secretly, like wrongs hushed-up, they went.
They were not ours:
We never heard to which front these were sent.

Nor there if they yet mock what women meant
Who gave them flowers.

Shall they return to beatings of great bells
In wild trainloads?

A few, a few, too few for drums and yells,
May creep back, silent, to still village wells
Up half-known roads.

John Betjeman

John Betjeman loved train travel. Railways feature in many of his poems as an integral part of the landscape and this love, coupled with that of Victorian architecture, led him to be a leading campaigner in the fight to preserve the Victorian heritage of Britain's railways. He fought unsuccessfully for the retention of the Doric Arch (or Propyleum) at Euston station in London, but his high-profile support for neighbouring St Pancras, coupled with a shift in public perception of Victorian architecture, helped to save that building. Today a statue of Betjeman stands at the refurbished St Pancras, staring in awe at the splendours all around.

'Pershore Station, or A Liverish Journey First Class' is one of Betjeman's most enduring train poems.

W. H. Auden

Released in 1936 by the Film Unit of the General Post Office (GPO), *Night Mail* was a documentary film showcasing the distribution of mail from London to Scotland via the London, Midland and Scottish Railway mail train. W. H. Auden wrote his famous poem 'Night Mail' specifically for this film – the rhythm of the verse echoed the sound of the train passing over the jointed track of the period.

Philip Larkin

One of the most well-loved railway poems ever written, published in 1964, Larkin's 'The Whitsun Weddings' describes a railway journey between Hull and London. The evocation of the sights and sounds of the journey is hard to beat.

RAILWAYS IN CHILDREN'S LITERATURE

Railways hold a special fascination for children and this is reflected in the many books published for them with a railway theme. For British readers, certainly, one of the most enduringly popular set of books is the *Railway Series* by the Reverend W. Awdry, a collection of titles based on the railways of the fictional island of Sodor, situated in the Irish Sea between the British mainland and the Isle of Man.

Originally written to cheer up his ailing son through a bout of measles, the first story in the series was published in 1945, was called *The Three Railway Engines* and introduced the characters of Edward, Gordon and Henry, as well as the *eminence grise* of the Sodor system, the Fat Director (who, we are told at the beginning of the third book, becomes the Fat Controller upon the nationalization of the railways).

The second book in the set introduces the character who becomes the figurehead for the entire series and whose name is now shorthand for a huge industry of books, merchandise and film – Thomas the Tank Engine.

It's not unreasonable to say that the books are now

creakingly out of date from a social point of view. It's true that Henry is bricked up inside a tunnel as a punishment for vanity (he's scared the rain will spoil his paintwork), the trucks are constantly bullied by the engines and female characters are conspicuous by their absence or are simpering characters like Thomas's coaches Annie and Clarabel. All of this notwithstanding, Thomas events at preserved railway companies produce huge crowds and the stories still provide happy memories for countless children.

Catering for a slightly older readership, E. Nesbit's novel *The Railway Children* (1906) is another much-loved story with an appeal that has endured for several generations. A touching tale of three children whose father has been imprisoned for spying and who move to a house close to a rural railway line, it has become a true classic across genres. It has been filmed for television in the UK four times and the 1970 film adaptation starring Dinah Sheridan, Bernard Cribbins and Jenny Agutter is a perennial favourite. The story has also reached a whole new audience thanks to theatre performances across the country, most notably featuring a real steam locomotive at the National Railway Museum, York, at the former Eurostar terminal at London Waterloo and most recently at a venue close to London King's Cross.

DARK DAYS

QUINTINSHILL

THE WORST RAIL INCIDENT in British history was the Quintinshill rail disaster, which occurred on 22 May 1915. Five trains were involved in this horror and the design of the railway carriages of the time contributed to the death toll.

Quintinshill was a signalbox near Gretna Green, situated on the Caledonian Railway line between Carlisle and Glasgow (today this is part of the West Coast Main Line). A troop train carrying soldiers to Liverpool for embarkation on to a ship to take them to Gallipoli crashed into a local train that had been left on the line in front of it. An express travelling in the other direction then crashed into the wreckage. The old (even for the period) wooden coaches were lit by gas held in tanks slung underneath their bodies. These ruptured and the gas caught fire. The flames spread rapidly, even engulfing two goods trains standing on parallel tracks. Officially 214 people died (although exact numbers are disputed) and 246 were injured, but some bodies were so badly burnt that they were never recovered or identified. Most of the dead came from the 7th Battalion of the Royal Scots.

In the enquiry that followed, it was found that lax working practices at Quintinshill signalbox started the chain of events that led to the disaster. The local train that had been shunted on to the main line had been forgotten about – the accepted procedures for reminding the signalmen that it was there had not been carried out.

HARROW & WEALDSTONE

There was a strange echo of the Quintinshill crash in the next biggest disaster to take place on Britain's railways. On the morning of 8 October 1952, at Harrow & Wealdstone in the north London suburbs, an express from Scotland ploughed into the back of a local train that had stopped at the station. As at Quintinshill, another train heading north then crashed into the wreckage, causing 112 people to die. Unlike the Scottish disaster, where it was clear that the signalmen had been at fault, at Harrow the signalling was working as it should have been – the Scottish express passed one signal at caution and another two at danger before hitting the local. As both the driver and fireman of that train were killed in the crash it has never been possible to ascertain exactly what happened.

The Harrow disaster put into stark relief the fact that even with signalling working as it should, human error could still lead to a major catastrophe. At the time, British Railways was developing a system that would give an additional warning to train crew if they passed a signal at danger and automatically apply the brakes if the crew did not respond. Harrow gave the additional impetus needed to get this implemented as soon as possible. Known as the Automatic Warning System (AWS), it was widely adopted, although as it relies on drivers paying full attention when overriding the warnings it isn't a completely failsafe system. A further development, the Train Protection and Warning System (TPWS) is designed to limit and control the impact of such errors.

MOORGATE

On the London Underground, the incident with the highest loss of life was the Moorgate Tube crash, which occurred on 28 February 1975 on the Northern City line, now a part of the National Rail commuter network out to Welwyn Garden City and Hertford but then worked as a short stub of the Northern line between Moorgate and Drayton Park. A Northern line train entered one of the terminus platforms at Moorgate at speed, entered the short overrun tunnel at the end of the platform and crashed into the buffers and end wall. The Northern City Line had been built to take full-size trains but because the line at that time was being operated by much smaller Tube trains, the force of the collision and the space above the train in the end tunnel meant that the front carriage was forced up and the second carriage was propelled beneath it. Forty-three people died. As at Harrow, the driver of the train was among the victims and as the signalling was working correctly it will never be known what caused the driver to fail to slow down. After the crash, new safety mechanisms were put in place on the Underground to halt trains if they enter terminal platforms and do not slow down sufficiently.

HATFIELD

In the five years between 1997 and 2002, there were four major accidents on Britain's railways – Southall, Ladbroke Grove, Hatfield and Potters Bar. Of all of these, the Hatfield accident had the biggest repercussions for the network.

The Hatfield rail crash on 17 October 2000 was the result of a rail breaking underneath the strain of a train passing over it at 185 km/h (115 mph). Four people were killed and the accident led to months of disruption across the entire network, as it became apparent that the incumbent track authority, Railtrack, was unable to confirm how many other areas might be at risk of a similar failure. This led to the application of more than 1,000 emergency speed limits around the country, some as low as 32 km/h (20 mph), leading to widespread chaos. Railtrack itself suffered the ultimate penalty – its share value plummeted when its costs spiralled as a result of both the penalties it had to pay and the extra, unplanned maintenance it had to carry out. Public support drained away and the company was finally forced into administration by the then Secretary of State for Transport, Stephen Byers.

CRASHES IN THE REST OF THE WORLD

The numbers killed in some individual British railway disasters have been high, but sadly there have been accidents around the world that have resulted in greater loss of life.

In France, the worst accident occurred in December 1917 when a train full of troops heading home derailed as its brakes failed while descending into a valley after crossing into France from Italy. The train came off the rails at St-Michel-de-Maurienne and burst into flames. The overall number of deaths is disputed – 425 bodies were officially identified but there was no way of knowing how many people had got on or off the train en route before the accident. Other bodies were burned beyond recognition and some of the wounded died later in hospital, so the total deaths were significantly higher.

In the United States, 1918 was a black year for railroad

accidents. In Nashville, Tennessee, on 9 July, two trains were involved in a head-on collision, resulting in at least 101 fatalities. Later that year, on 1 November in Brooklyn, New York City, a train on the Brighton Beach Line of the Brooklyn Rapid Transit Company took a corner at a speed far above the official restriction. The wooden-bodied train derailed and some of the cars sustained severe damage. At least ninety-three people died in the crash, which became known as the Malbone Street Wreck.

Railway accidents can happen for all sorts of reasons, from equipment failure to natural disasters to human error. Excessive speed was responsible for two recent disasters in different parts of the world. On 24 July 2013, on the approach to Santiago de Compostela station in north-western Spain, a high-speed train failed to slow for a curve, taking it approximately twice as fast as the speed limit allowed. The train derailed and seventy-nine people were killed. Since the accident, additional safety features have been added to the tracks in the approach to the location, ensuring that brakes are automatically applied in cases of excessive speed.

On 13 May 2015, an Amtrak train travelling between Washington and New York derailed in Philadelphia, killing eight people. It, too, entered a curve at around twice the speed limit. At the time of writing investigations as to the cause of the accident are still ongoing, with calls for additional safety equipment to be installed.

The rail disaster with the highest number of deaths overall happened as the result of a natural phenomenon. On 26

December 2004, a train travelling between Colombo and Galle, in Sri Lanka, was struck by tsunami waves generated by the undersea earthquake that had occurred off the coast of Sumatra earlier that day. At least 1,700 people died in the rail disaster, with many bodies swept away and never found.

CRIMINALS ON THE RAILWAY

Disasters, while shocking, are thankfully extremely rare on the railways. A more common threat is that posed by criminals who target those travelling by train. Railways offered fertile ground for criminals – from pickpockets at stations, preying on distracted travellers, to serious crimes of violence undertaken in the closed compartments that were common for so long. The first murder on a train in Britain occurred in 1864, when Franz Muller killed Thomas Briggs on a North London Railway service.

The murder of Thomas Briggs led to calls for increased safety aboard trains with closed compartments. This led to the development of the communication cord, allowing passengers to alert staff in an emergency.

THE GREAT TRAIN ROBBERY

Of course, criminals don't always target passengers. The Great Train Robbery took place in the early hours of 8 August 1963 and involved the overnight Glasgow to London mail train. It had left Glasgow the previous night at 6.50 p.m. and consisted of twelve carriages staffed by General Post Office (GPO) employees. At Sears Crossing, Ledburn, Buckinghamshire, the gang of fifteen robbers had tampered with the signals by covering the green aspect and using a battery to illuminate the red. The train, driven by Driver Jack Mills with David Whitby as secondman, came to a stand at the spurious signal at around 3 a.m. Whitby climbed down to call the signalman from a trackside telephone but discovered that the cables had been cut. On returning to the train, he was grabbed and overpowered by one of the criminal gang. Other gang members entered the cab of the train and in the struggle Driver Mills was struck by a cosh and additionally banged his head on the instrument panel of the locomotive.

Now that they had stopped the train, the robbers then had to move it to a nearby bridge, from where they could transfer the money they were after into a waiting van. As part of the planning for the robbery, one member of the gang had spent some time befriending railway staff and getting an idea of how things worked, in the hope that they would be able to move the train without needing someone with the specialist skill. In the end, the gang did recruit a former train driver but they hit a snag as it turned out that he had no experience with the new type of diesel locomotive at the head of this particular train. So the gang had no alternative but to force the injured Driver Mills to move the train the 800 m (half a mile) or so up the track to Bridego Bridge.

Once at the bridge, the robbers identified and targeted the vehicle known as the High Value Packages carriages – on the day of the robbery this contained bags holding cash to the value of £2.5–£3 million. The onboard staff tried to resist the intruders but were overwhelmed and made to lie down on the floor of the carriage.

It took in the region of twenty minutes for the robbers to remove 120 sacks and load them into their truck. They then made their getaway in a pair of waiting Land Rovers through country lanes to their initial hideout at Leatherslade Farm, Buckinghamshire. Here they divided up the loot and each member of the gang received in the region of £150,000 (the equivalent of over £2.5 million at today's values).

Back at the railway, the alarm had been raised and the police began communicating the robbery on their radios.

From then it was a game of cat and mouse with the police. The gang were able to listen in on police radios, so could hear how the search was going. They realized that the police would close in quickly so they organized cars to enable them to leave the farm sooner than they had intended.

A major police operation was put into place around the scene of the crime and five days after the robbery, following a local tip-off, the police arrived at Leatherslade Farm and gleaned valuable evidence. This, coupled with a wide-ranging investigation, eventually led to the capture of eight of the main gang later in 1963. The leader, Bruce Reynolds, wasn't captured until 1968. Ronald 'Buster' Edwards gave himself up in 1966.

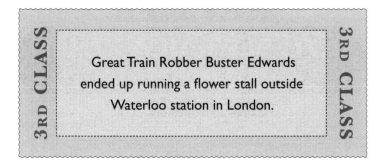

3RD CLASS

Great Train Robber Buster Edwards ended up running a flower stall outside Waterloo station in London.

3RD CLASS

The robber who became the highest-profile member of the gang in later years was Ronald Biggs. Sentenced to thirty years in prison, he escaped in 1965 and fled abroad, first to Sydney, Australia, then on to Melbourne and eventually ending up in Brazil. There he was safe because there was no extradition treaty at that time between Brazil and the United Kingdom.

Eventually, after a high-profile life in Brazil, Biggs finally indicated that he would be willing to return voluntarily to the UK – he arrived in 2001 and was immediately sent back to prison. Biggs was released on compassionate grounds in 2009 and he died in December 2013.

NOTABLE RAILWAYMEN (AND ANIMALS)

GEORGE HUDSON

GEORGE HUDSON WAS BORN in Yorkshire in 1800. He later received a huge (for the time) bequest of £30,000 from his great-uncle, in gratitude for Hudson's solicitude during his final illness. Using this money to gain influence, Hudson rose to become Lord Mayor of York in 1837. In 1845 he was elected as the Conservative Member of Parliament for Sunderland.

Hudson became involved in the promotion and direction of railway companies, using his money, influence and position as an MP to steamroller his personal interests through, often using extremely shady methods. Despite this, his nickname, 'the Railway King', demonstrated just how deeply involved he was with the development of railways in the north and east of England. He was the quintessential railway baron, pushing through schemes at the height of the railway mania in Britain. For years his methods were, if not condoned, mainly accepted.

Eventually, of course, it all unravelled. Hudson had interests in various railway companies converging on York but he didn't control the new Great Northern line that arrived from the south and offered a much quicker way to London than via the Midland Railway, of which Hudson was chairman. Unfortunately for him, he was also chairman of two other railway companies, including the York, Newcastle and Berwick, which would benefit greatly from the new, quicker route offered by the Great Northern. Faced with an impossible dilemma, Hudson agreed that the Great Northern could use his existing line into York rather than building its own. This clearly gave the new company instant and much cheaper access to York over the same line used by the much longer Midland route.

The board of the Midland Railway were quite understandably furious. Forced to resign his chairmanship, Hudson was then called to account by one of his other companies, the York and North Midland Railway. Things snowballed, similar questions were asked by his other companies, and eventually a parliamentary enquiry found that he had abused his position to further his own interest. In 1865, he was imprisoned in York for debt, but was released later that year after the debt was paid off by a friend. Other debts remained, though. Hudson fled abroad but returned the following year, only to be arrested and imprisoned again.

On being allowed to leave prison to visit his lawyer, Hudson took the opportunity to flee again but this time a group of his friends got together and started a protected trust fund, providing an income that couldn't be drawn upon by his railway creditors.

Hudson returned to Britain in 1870 – the Debtors' Act 1869 had abolished imprisonment for debt – but by this time his health had suffered irretrievably and he died in London on 14 December 1871.

In the age-old discussion around 'Does the end justify the means?', George Hudson's business life could be a textbook example. Undoubtedly a blustering rogue and a crook, many of the railways he forced through at the time are still with us today and form a valuable part of the national network. Indeed, not everything bequeathed by Hudson was the product of a dodgy deal. He understood that the various railway companies operating in the middle of the nineteenth century needed to have a structure to enable them to work cohesively as a network. Key to this was the need to ensure that passengers could have as seamless a journey as possible, even if that journey involved travel on the trains of more than one company.

The London and Birmingham Railway had put forward the idea of a Railway Clearing House, a body that would take the income from all tickets bought across all railway companies and allocate the revenue correctly according to the journeys actually made. This would ensure that a passenger could buy one ticket for a journey and not have to worry about rebooking en route or encountering difficulties when changing trains. It would also have a similar responsibility to examine goods traffic and apportion revenue accordingly. George Hudson was a huge supporter of this concept and did what he could to push it through. The Railway Clearing House was launched in January 1842.

RAILWAY TIME

The Railway Clearing House later became instrumental in getting Greenwich Mean Time adopted by railway companies throughout the country. Prior to the advent of railways, different communities around the country had their own time – Bristol, for example, was ten minutes behind Greenwich Mean Time. The Great Western Railway had been the first adopter of a standardized railway time based on GMT, recognizing the problems caused in timetabling and the potential confusion in the minds of passengers. There was also a very real risk to safety.

The RCH decreed in 1847 that all railway companies should adopt Railway Time. This wasn't an overnight process but by 1855 the majority of towns and cities in the country had converted – the recently implemented telegraph system was used to send time signals from Greenwich across the land.

THOMAS EDMONDSON

Clearly, if you're going to have a central body like the Railway Clearing House to apportion revenue then you need a standardized system of recording that revenue. Until the setting up of the RCH, railway tickets had been a hit-and-miss affair. Consisting of varying scraps of paper written out by ticket clerks and not always fully accounted for, they were a paradise for fraudulent activity. Thomas Edmondson, a stationmaster on the Newcastle and Carlisle Railway, came up with the idea of pre-printed cardboard tickets with consecutive serial numbers that were date-stamped on issue. He later patented a machine that could print these in batches and charged royalties to railway companies for their use. It was a simple yet effective system and it made him a rich man. Edmondson card tickets were exported to railway companies around the world and continued to be issued in Britain right up until 1989.

GEORGE BRADSHAW

Once you have your new-fangled Edmondson ticket then you'll need something to tell you what time your train will leave. As with other elements of early railway travel, the individual companies provided their own public timetables to their own, varying designs. As the network grew rapidly, a more efficient method was needed to show timings throughout the country and across all companies.

George Bradshaw (interestingly, like Thomas Edmondson, a Quaker) was a publisher and map-maker born in Salford in 1801. He had already published a guide to the canals of Lancashire and Yorkshire but in 1839 he published his first guide to railways and this quickly developed into a monthly publication. Soon seen as indispensable, *Bradshaw's* was an early example of a brand name that became used interchangeably to mean any railway timetable, in the way that a Hoover is popularly used for any vacuum cleaner today. Publication continued right up to 1961, although the popularity and utility had waned since the railway companies had consolidated into ever-larger units at the Grouping in 1923 and then into British Railways on nationalization in 1948. Bradshaw himself died of cholera in 1853, on a visit to Norway, and is buried close to Oslo Cathedral. Although no longer produced as a guide to current railways, *Bradshaw's* has recently experience a surge of popularity in Britain thanks to the BBC television series *Great Railway Journeys*, in which former politician Michael Portillo toured the country with an original copy, visiting places named in the guide. Several facsimile editions of both guides and maps are now available, although original copies can command extremely high prices.

SIR NIGEL GRESLEY

If you ask the average person in the street to name a steam locomotive, the chances are that they will come up with either *Flying Scotsman* or *Mallard*. Both of these iconic locomotives were designed by the same man – Sir Nigel Gresley.

Herbert Nigel Gresley was born in 1876 and served his engineering apprenticeship at the London and North Western Railway works in Crewe. He later moved to the Lancashire and Yorkshire Railway, based at Horwich in Lancashire, but it was in 1905 that he took up a position in the railway environment that was to make his name – the Great Northern Railway (today, roughly speaking, the portion of the East Coast main line between London and York, plus branches). He rose to become Chief Mechanical Engineer in 1911 and at the time of the Grouping in 1923 became CME of the newly formed London and North Eastern Railway.

Before even considering his achievements in steam locomotive design, it's worth pointing out that Nigel Gresley was also a pioneer in coaching stock. By the early twentieth century, complaints were being received about the rough-riding of the

six-wheeled carriages of the East Coast Joint Stock. This was a pool of carriages owned jointly by the three railway companies that ran the line up the east coast from London to Scotland – the Great Northern, as far as York; the North Eastern from York to Berwick-upon-Tweed and the North British from Berwick to Edinburgh and beyond.

The solution pioneered by Gresley in 1907 was to set two carriage bodies upon three bogies – i.e. one at each end of the pair of carriages and one in the middle straddling both of them. This is known as articulation and resulted in cheaper construction (only three bogies per pair of coaches instead of four) with a concomitant weight saving and much improved ride quality over the previous six-wheeled carriages.

Gresley continued to use articulation for later stock builds, notably for his 'quad-art' suburban sets and for his prestige express coaches built in 1935–7 for the Silver Jubilee and Coronation services. The disadvantage of articulation, of course, is that you have to keep trains in rigidly formed sets, as you can't split articulated coaches. This was one of the reasons why the concept didn't really catch on hugely elsewhere although it certainly hasn't gone away. Many light railway vehicles (e.g. trams) around the world use articulation and one of the most high-profile uses from a British perspective is on the Eurostar train sets, linking London with Brussels and Paris.

But of course Nigel Gresley's pre-eminence in railway history is due to his steam locomotive designs. He had already produced several highly regarded locomotive classes before he turned his attention to new express 'Pacific' locomotives for the east coast route. The first of the new Class A1 locomotives was outshopped from the Great Northern Railway works at Doncaster in 1922. This was named, not perhaps unsurprisingly, *Great Northern* and given the number 1470. Production continued, with a fellow locomotive also being completed in the same year and another ten authorized by the GNR. These were still under construction at the time of the Grouping and were therefore completed under the auspices of the London and North Eastern Railway. No one today remembers poor old locomotive 1471 (*Sir Frederick Banbury* for those who are interested) but loco 1472 went on to inspire worldwide fame and affection.

Flying Scotsman

Completed in 1923, the locomotive was chosen to represent the London and North Eastern Railway at the British Empire Exhibition at Wembley in 1924. To this end it was renumbered 4472 and named *Flying Scotsman*, after the unofficial name of the regular daytime express service then running between London and Edinburgh, with trains leaving both cities at 10 a.m. on their respective journeys. This was officially known as the *Special Scotch Express* and had been running since 1862. In 1924, the LNER made the nickname of the service official to match that of the locomotive, in what we would now call a branding exercise.

In 1928, the locomotive was one of a pool chosen to run the new, accelerated, non-stop London to Edinburgh *Flying*

Scotsman service and in 1934, 4472 became the first locomotive officially recorded as running at 160 km/h (100 mph). (The Great Western had claimed this record for their locomotive *City of Truro* as far back as 1904 but this had never been officially recognized, leading to disputes among partisan rail fans ever since.)

Renumbered after the Second World War, *Flying Scotsman* became (very briefly) 502, then 103, though this was also a short-lived number as on nationalization all steam locomotives had to be renumbered to avoid duplication. Numbers of the locomotives of the London and North Eastern Railway were increased by 60,000, so our hero ended up as 60103.

The fifties were a fairly uneventful time but when British Railways announced in 1962 that *Flying Scotsman* was to be withdrawn, businessman Alan Pegler stepped in and bought it. After heavy investment, the locomotive was sent in 1969 on a long tour of the US and Canada. Unfortunately, during this tour, the money ran out and *Flying Scotsman* ended up impounded at San Francisco Docks. It was only the intervention of William MacAlpine, who bought the locomotive and paid off the fees, that saw it return to the UK.

In 1988, *Flying Scotsman* went travelling again, this time to Australia. During that tour, the locomotive met up with an old companion – Great Western Railway 4079 *Pendennis Castle*. Both locomotives had been displayed next to each other at the second British Empire Exhibition in 1925. *Pendennis Castle* had been bought by a mining company and exported to Australia in the seventies for use on heritage excursion trips on that company's lines.

Returning to the UK, the locomotive settled down to a spell working main-line excursions for enthusiasts, but trouble was never far away. A progression of financial problems followed until in 2004 it was bought by the National Railway Museum in York and became part of the National Collection. Its difficulties hadn't ended, though – at the time of writing it is the subject of a long and protracted restoration project involving spiralling costs due to an increasing number of faults that need to be rectified. Current projections are that it will return to service some time in 2015.

For Christmas 1931, the London and North Eastern Railway served Christmas lunch on the *Flying Scotsman* and presents were provided for the children on the sleeping-car trains. How Father Christmas would have delivered them remains a mystery . . .

The Gresley A4s

The routes from London to Scotland, via the west or the east coast, have always been fertile grounds for speed races and competition. The golden age for such competition was the 1930s, when both the LMS and the LNER vied with one another to produce the most lavish trains and the fastest schedules on their respective routes.

Leader in the field was Sir Nigel Gresley. He had visited Germany in 1933 and had been very favourably impressed by the high-speed, diesel-powered train known as the *Fliegender Hamburger* ('Flying Hamburger'), introduced that year. He knew, however, that diesel technology wasn't at that time capable of hauling the heavy expresses run on his railway and he determined to create a class of steam locomotives that would do the job.

In 1935, the first of his A4 Pacific locomotives was introduced – eventually they became a class of thirty-five, all built between 1935 and 1938. The first four were used to inaugurate a streamlined service between London and Newcastle known as the Silver Jubilee, in honour of George V's twenty-five years on the throne. Other streamlined services were introduced – the Coronation between London and Edinburgh in 1937 and named for the coronation of King George VI, and the West Riding Limited between London and Bradford/Leeds.

The A4s went on to perform exceptionally, hammering up and down the east coast main line right up to the introduction of diesels in the early sixties. They had one last triumphant period, though – a number in Scotland were allocated to operate the demanding Glasgow to Aberdeen expresses, which had been retimed in 1962 to run in three hours – thirty minutes faster than previously. Given the opportunity to run these beautiful machines up to their retirement, the Scottish crews lost no time in producing a succession of sparkling, high-speed runs.

But of course, the stand-out achievement of both Sir Nigel Gresley and of his A4 class was the world speed record for steam. On 3 July 1938, 4468 *Mallard*, driven by Joseph Duddington and fired by Thomas Bray, hit 202.8 km/h (126 mph) on a test run between Grantham and Peterborough. The record stands to this day.

Unlike *Flying Scotsman*, which is the sole representative of its class left, there are six preserved A4s. One, *Dwight D. Eisenhower*, is in the National Railroad Museum in Green Bay, Wisconsin. Another, *Dominion of Canada*, is in the Canadian Railway Museum in Saint-Constant, Quebec, and the other four are preserved at various locations in Britain. *Mallard* is not currently operational but the remaining three are currently cleared for use on the main line – *Bittern*, *Union of South Africa* and, fittingly, *Sir Nigel Gresley*.

WILLIAM STANIER

The rivalry between the east and west coast routes from London to Scotland had been intense since the nineteenth century. Unofficial races had taken place and huge efforts were being made to produce locomotives and rolling stock that could tempt people from one company to the other.

While Nigel Gresley was busy designing and constructing his A4s at Doncaster for the London and North Eastern, William Stanier was hard at work at Crewe, designing the London, Midland and Scottish Railway's response.

Stanier was born in Swindon and started out on the Great Western Railway in that town, becoming chief assistant to the then Chief Mechanical Engineer Charles Collett before moving to the LMS in 1932. He found a company in dire need of heavier locomotives for both passengers and freight, so using techniques and features learned at the Great Western he quickly introduced a fleet of strong, reliable locomotives, including the mixed traffic 'Black Five' 4-6-0 class and the heavy freight '8F' 2-8-0 class.

Impressive though these locomotives were, however, if the LMS were to compete with the LNER Stanier would have to come up with a design to beat the Gresley Pacifics. He introduced a small class of his own Pacifics, the Princess Royals – thirteen locomotives between 1933 and 1935 – but he is best remembered for developing this concept into his masterwork: the Princess Coronation class. The first five were built at Crewe for the inauguration of the Coronation Scot service and, in the spirit of the age, were clad in streamlined casing. Painted blue with silver stripes that extended all the way down the train they were a stirring sight, although it's debatable just how much the streamlining helped. Certainly they seemed a lot bulkier than the greyhound appearance of Gresley's A4s.

All of that notwithstanding, the Princess Coronations were the most powerful steam locomotives ever built in Britain and in 1937, on a test run, the first locomotive 6220 *Coronation* achieved a record speed of 183 km/h (114 mph), beating the previous record held by the LNER. As we've seen, of course, the LNER's *Mallard* went on to smash that record the following year but it does demonstrate how closely matched the two companies were in this field.

In all, thirty-eight Princess Coronations were built. Only the first ten were streamlined after it was found that in day-to-day service it didn't do anything to help performance and indeed hindered maintenance. After many years, the decision was taken to restore streamlining to the preserved locomotive *Duchess of Hamilton* – at the time of writing this can be seen at the National Railway Museum in York, resplendent in the later red and gold colour scheme. The Duchesses represented the pinnacle of Stanier's career and indeed, for some, the pinnacle of British locomotive design, given their power. He was knighted in 1943 and died after a long retirement in 1965.

OLIVER BULLEID

The phrase 'mercurial genius' might have been invented for Oliver Bulleid, the man who became the Chief Mechanical Engineer of the Southern Railway in 1937 and lasted in the post until nationalization in 1948.

Bulleid's first completely new design for the Southern was authorized in 1938. This was to be a completely new design of express passenger locomotive – a 4-6-2 Pacific but with a host of new ideas, many based on what he had seen of locomotive design on the Continent. Unfortunately, war intervened. The priority for the railways was to move freight, troops and equipment – they couldn't be seen to be producing new, express passenger locomotives when the need was for engines that could pull all sorts of trains (known as 'mixed traffic' engines). This didn't stop Bulleid, though. He simply referred to his new engines as 'mixed traffic' and got them through.

Known as the Merchant Navy class (they were gradually given the names of the various shipping companies that served the Southern's ports), Bulleid's first thirty Pacifics were revolutionary for a number of reasons. They were the first Pacifics to run on the Southern; they were covered with an 'air-smoothed' casing, giving them a very distinct appearance; they had a unique chain-driven valve gear encased in an oil bath; electric lighting was fitted along with a number of improvements to the driving cab, designed to make things easier and safer for the driver and fireman; and their wheels were of an unusual design known as

Bulleid Firth Brown. Not all of these innovations were ultimately successful, however. The valve gear and oil bath gave enormous trouble in particular, and in some cases oil leaks led to locomotives catching fire. Overall modifications were made constantly to improve the design, both pre- and post-nationalization. Undaunted, after the first batch of thirty Merchant Navy Pacifics had been constructed, Bulleid introduced a second batch of similar, yet lighter Pacifics. These eventually numbered 110 locomotives and were intended to operate over lines, principally in the West Country, where the heavier Merchant Navies couldn't run. Because of the high maintenance regimes needed to keep the Bulleid Pacifics running, thought was given to scrapping the whole class in the 1950s. However, due to the excellence of the Bulleid boiler and the fact that when all was well the engines could perform very efficiently, the decision was taken to rebuild them into a more conventional engine, keeping the successful elements such as the electric lighting, effective boiler and BFB wheels, yet ditching the more revolutionary aspects as well as the air-smoothed casing. The first rebuilt engine appeared in 1956 and all of the Merchant Navies were remodelled by 1960, although fifty of the Light Pacifics were spared rebuilding when the programme ended in 1961. By that time, the writing was on the wall for steam traction and it was not deemed viable to continue with the programme. As it was, once the Southern took the decision to scrap steam by 1967, some rebuilt engines, excellent machines though they were, had only given six or seven years' service.

The British Double-Decker Train

Bulleid's idiosyncrasies didn't stop with steam locomotive design. Faced with ever-increasing passenger numbers on the commuter lines from south-east London into Charing Cross and Cannon Street, he came up with an idea for double-decker trains. Unfortunately, as we've seen in the chapter on railway loading gauges, the British railway system wasn't built with enough clearance for genuine double-decker trains. Bulleid came up with a kind of one-and-a-half-decker arrangement – where stairs led up from individual compartments to others just above – resulting in cramped accommodation all round. Worse, the design of the trains with just one door leading to both upper and lower compartments meant that loading and unloading times were unacceptably prolonged. Only two 'double-decker' trains were ever built but surprisingly for a failed concept they lasted quite a long time. Introduced in 1949 they lived out their lives on the south-eastern suburban lines they were built for, between London and Dartford, until 1971. British Rail decided that the answer to increasing capacity was to lengthen trains instead.

Leader of the Pack?

In a career spent pushing the envelope of design, Bulleid produced some excellent work. His new carriages for long-distance services were heavily influential on later carriage design, for example. Unfortunately, he also came up with some designs that just didn't work – the most striking example being his development of a new locomotive known as the *Leader*.

Conceived as an attempt to bring the steam locomotive into the modern age and to compete with the up-and-coming diesel locomotives, the *Leader* incorporated a large number of technical innovations. To the non-specialist, however, the most striking thing about the class was its appearance. Traditional steam locomotives are driven from the cab, so that the driver has to look past the entire length of the boiler to see the view ahead. The *Leader* had cabs at both front and back, similar to most diesels and to the modern electric locomotives introduced by the Southern.

Construction began on the prototype in 1947, at the Southern's Brighton Works. The completed locomotive emerged in 1949 (by now in the nationalized world) and testing out on the main line began straightaway. Unfortunately, trials were a disaster in most respects. Although the boiler performed well, consumption of coal and water was high. Working conditions for both driver and fireman were said to be excessively hot and mechanically there were many failures. Sadly for Bulleid, the nationalized, post-war British Railways had neither the resources nor the inclination to spend on fixing the various faults with the design and the whole project was scrapped in 1951. Bulleid died in 1970 but it is a fitting tribute to the design of his locomotives that of the 140 Pacifics built, thirty-one still exist today, in varying states of preservation.

COLONEL HOLMAN F. STEPHENS

One of the most idiosyncratic figures in British railway history was Colonel Holman Fred Stephens. Originally an apprentice to the Metropolitan Railway, he later worked on the construction of the Cranbrook and Paddock Wood Railway in Kent, which opened in 1892. A couple of years later he became an associate member of the Institution of Civil Engineers, which allowed him to get on with what became a lifetime's project to build light railway lines into sparsely populated rural areas.

The Light Railways Act of 1896 had been introduced after a period of economic hardship and was intended to make it easier to open rural railways, for the transport of both people and, especially, goods. Prior to this legislation, each new railway line had to have its own Act of Parliament – as may be imagined, this added to the cost and time it took to bring each line into use. Accordingly, rural areas of sparse population tended to be ignored by the railway companies as not being worth the trouble.

Stephens reacted to the new Act with gusto. He had already built two railways – the 914mm (3ft) gauge Rye and Camber Tramway in East Sussex and the splendidly named Hundred of Manhood and Selsey Tramway, running south from Chichester to Selsey. Both of these railways were built as tramways, avoiding the need for the stricter engineering standards associated with railways prior to the 1896 Act. After the change of rules, Stephens built the Rother Valley Railway, which later became the Kent and East Sussex

Railway. Many others followed, including the East Kent Railway, the North Devon and Cornwall Junction Light Railway (between Bere Alston and Callington), the Sheppey Light Railway and the Shropshire and Montgomeryshire Railway.

Unfortunately, in many cases, Stephens' railways or indeed others that were built under the Light Railway Act were not a huge success. Running through sparsely populated countryside, sometimes far from the communities they purported to serve, they were hit hard by the development of road transport from the 1920s. Most fell into general disuse but it's heartening that at least part of the Kent and East Sussex and the East Kent Railway survive today in preservation. The K&ESR in particular is an expanding tourist attraction, running between Tenterden and Bodiam with aspirations to extend back through to Robertsbridge where it will link up with National Rail. Tenterden station plays host to a museum dedicated to Stephens' achievements.

The line between Bere Alston and Gunnislake survives as part of the National Rail system, linking as it does parts of Cornwall and Devon with poor road connections.

GEORGE CHURCHWARD AND CHARLES COLLETT

George Jackson Churchward was the Chief Mechanical Engineer of the Great Western Railway from 1902 to 1922. During his tenure at Swindon, he designed a succession of outstanding steam locomotives and instituted a system of standardized parts that could fit a whole range of different engines. Churchward also designed the City class of locomotives, built to the 4-4-0 wheel arrangement. One of this class, *City of Truro*, has long been claimed as the holder of the record for the first engine to surpass 160 km/h (100 mph), although this is disputed by some.

Churchward's successor at the Great Western, Charles Collett, took the decision to develop Churchward's designs and came up with a stable of locomotives including the Castle and the King class – iconic among railway enthusiasts – but Collett is generally seen as an engineer who developed, rather than innovated, steam locomotive design.

Churchward met an unfortunate end – he had retired in 1922 but continued to live close to his beloved Great Western Railway at Swindon. One day in 1933, short of sight and hard of hearing, he was inspecting what he thought might be a line fault when he was struck by an express heading for Fishguard.

Collett retired from the GWR in 1941 and died in 1952, aged eighty.

ROBERT RIDDLES

Upon nationalization on 1 January 1948, Britain's railways were still battered and exhausted by the destruction and lack of maintenance due to the Second World War. There were still thousands of old, pre-grouping steam locomotives slogging their way around the system and there was a dire need for new construction. Each of the Big Four had continued to construct their own locomotive designs right up to nationalization and this continued well into the nationalized period where construction had already been authorized and was under way.

Robert Riddles had come up through the London and North Western Railway to become the assistant to William Stanier at the London, Midland and Scottish Railway. Just prior to nationalization he had been appointed as the Member of the Railway Executive for Mechanical and Electrical Engineering. In this role, he and his team had been charged to come up with a range of standardized locomotive designs, of different sizes and power abilities, to enable easier and quicker maintenance. Many other railways in the world at that time were switching or had switched to electric or diesel traction. In Britain, though, coal was king – there were millions of tons of it in the ground and coal-mining was a huge part of British industry. Therefore new steam locomotive designs were seen as the most effective way forward.

In all, 999 British Railways Standard locomotives were built. In general they were well received, as they had been designed for easier maintenance and greater comfort for the crew. The last example, and the last steam locomotive to be built for British Railways, was 92220 *Evening Star*, outshopped from Swindon in 1960. By this time, however, official policy had changed once more. Steam was to be ousted at the earliest possible moment, to be replaced by diesel or electric locomotives. The transition was completed with indecent haste, with steam officially ending in 1968 (although it had disappeared from large parts of the country before that). Many of Riddles' excellent designs still had years of life left in them – *Evening Star*, for example, was withdrawn after only five years' service, representing a shocking waste of resources. Luckily, it was saved for posterity and is now part of the National Collection.

ANDRÉ CHAPELON

André Chapelon was a French engineer and locomotive designer, whose main contribution to steam technology was the rigour he brought to designing the most efficient locomotives possible. In the 1920s, together with the Finnish engineer Kyösti Kylälä, Chapelon designed the Kylchap exhaust system, bringing greater power output and increasing fuel and water efficiency.

The Kylchap exhaust system wasn't widely adopted, however, despite the proven benefits, although a fitting testament to the robustness and quality of the design may be the fact that *Mallard*, the fastest steam locomotive in history, had been equipped with a Kylchap exhaust.

RICHARD BEECHING

Few names in British railway history evoke quite as many opinions as that of Dr Richard Beeching. Born in Kent in 1913, Beeching went on to study Physics and gained his PhD at Imperial College, London. During the Second World War he worked on armaments design, continuing until 1948. That year he joined ICI.

In 1961, the then Minister of Transport, Ernest Marples, announced that Beeching had been seconded from ICI to be the first Chairman of the soon-to-be-created British Railways Board. This had taken over responsibility for railway operations from the British Transport Commission, set up on nationalization to look after railway, canal and road freight transport, as well as a much wider remit including docks, some bus operations, British Transport Police, the former railway hotels and a film unit, British Transport Films. The removal company Pickfords and the travel company Thomas Cook were also part of the BTC. By the end of the 1950s the BTC had been targeted for break-up by the government, to be replaced by a number of individual successor bodies.

Beeching's remit was to improve the finances of Britain's railways – at that time running with huge losses. The uncontrolled construction of railways in the nineteenth century had given rise to a network that contained a large number of duplicate lines as well as a number of lines serving places that would never provide enough traffic to turn a profit. Many lines were slow, circuitous and had stations far from the communities they purported to serve. The advent of motor buses in the early years of the twentieth century ensured that in many cases local railways became an irrelevance to their potential passenger base. The network had reached its zenith in 1914 and since then had shrunk as the first completely hopeless lines began to close. A further obstacle to turning a profit was that the railways in Britain were designated as common carriers, which meant that they were obliged to carry any freight load offered to them at a nationally agreed price, whether or not that price enabled them to make a profit. This was a clear handicap and the common carrier requirement was abolished in the Transport Act 1962 (the same act that abolished the British Transport Commission and led to the creation of the British Railways Board.)

Beeching's solution was published in 1963 as a report entitled *The Reshaping of Britain's Railways*. In it, he proposed the closure of around 2,300 stations and 8,000 km (5,000 miles) of lines. To help deal with the losses incurred in the freight operation he proposed that the network should concentrate on coal and minerals and the introduction of a system of containerization, running trains as bulk point-to-point carriers and eliminating the costly and time-consuming practice of shunting wagons at multiple locations on a route. These container trains formed the genesis of today's Freightliner network.

Beeching published a second report in 1965 in which he proposed investment in a core of main routes along with the abandonment of others. Proposals included the concentration of all Anglo-Scottish services up the West Coast Main Line, closing the East Coast route north of Newcastle. There would be no service west of Plymouth and no railways in Wales other than the main line to Swansea. There would be nothing to the north or west of Aberdeen in Scotland. By this time the Labour government of Harold Wilson was in place and the plans in this second report were rejected. Beeching's secondment ended early and he returned to ICI in June 1965.

Many of the proposals in the first Beeching report were accepted and many, but not all, of the recommended lines were closed. Clearly circumstances were very different in the early sixties but the extraordinary recent growth in rail travel in Britain in recent years has led to calls for some of the closed lines to be reopened, despite the huge difficulties involved (repurchase of the track bed, redevelopment in the way and so on).

HEROES IN ADVERSITY: RAILWAYMEN AWARDED THE GEORGE CROSS

Norman Tunna

Norman Tunna worked for the Great Western Railway in Birkenhead, Cheshire (today part of Merseyside).

On 26 September 1940, the German Luftwaffe carried out a bombing raid on the Mersey docks. As well as bombs, many incendiary devices were dropped, resulting in fires on both dock and railway property. In the midst of the havoc, Norman Tunna discovered a fire in a wagon containing explosive materials. Despite the obvious danger to life, Tunna extinguished the fire and made the wagon safe.

As part of a programme of locomotive namings to remember railway heroes, a diesel locomotive was named *Norman Tunna GC* in 1982.

Benjamin Gimbert and James Nightall

Benjamin Gimbert and James William Nightall were, respectively, a driver and fireman working for the London and North Eastern Railway. On 2 June 1944, they were on the footplate of an ammunition train. As they arrived at Soham station in Cambridgeshire, Gimbert discovered that the wagon next to the engine, full of ammunition, was on fire. Gimbert asked Nightall to try to uncouple the burning wagon from the train, so that he could then draw it clear from the rest of the ammunition. Nightall complied immediately, all the while knowing that the wagon could explode at any time.

Nightall rejoined Gimbert and the locomotive drew the burning wagon away from the rest of the train. As they came close to the signalbox, the wagon finally exploded, demolishing the station buildings and killing James Nightall outright. The signalman in the box at the time died later but driver Gimbert survived, despite being lacerated by flying glass and other debris.

Benjamin Gimbert died on 6 May 1976 and in 1981 two diesel locomotives were named in memory of both men.

John Axon

John Axon was the driver in charge of a steam-hauled freight train from Buxton to Warrington on 9 February 1957. As the train approached a steep downward gradient, the pipe leading to the brake fractured, letting loose a gush of high pressure, scalding steam directly at Axon. Despite being badly burnt, he battled, along with the fireman, to get the train under control by using the handbrake. The fireman then leapt off the train to try to apply as many brakes as he could to the individual wagons, all to no avail. Driver Axon continued to do what he could in his cab but nothing could stop the train as it descended the gradient.

Sadly, before anything else could be done, the train crashed into another freight train on the line ahead of it. Driver Axon was killed, age fifty-six.

In keeping with the tradition of naming locomotives after employees awarded the GC in the course of their duties, a locomotive (this time electric) was named *Driver John Axon GC* in 1981.

Wallace Arnold Oakes

Driver Wallace Oakes was in charge of a steam-hauled passenger train on 5 June 1965. The train left Crewe and about seven miles into its journey the engine suffered a blow-back – a hugely dangerous phenomenon in which flames and smoke are forced back and out of the firehole into the cab of the locomotive.

The fireman managed to climb out of the cab (the train

had been travelling at around 96 km/h or 60 mph at the time) and rubbed his burning clothing along the side of the locomotive to extinguish it. He remained clinging to the side of the locomotive, sensing that the brakes had been applied, until the train came to a halt. When he climbed back into the cab, Driver Oakes was no longer there – on looking out of the train, he saw him lying by the track, severely burnt all over his body.

Later investigation found that Driver Oakes had stayed at his position, despite the flames, and had applied the brakes and carried out the other procedures necessary to make the locomotive safe.

Driver Oakes sustained burns over 80 per cent of his body. He survived for a week in a Manchester hospital but died on 12 June. An electric locomotive was named *Driver Wallace Oakes GC* in 1981.

James Kennedy

James Kennedy was a Security Officer working at British Rail Engineering Ltd, Glasgow, Scotland.

On 21 December 1973, six armed men carried out a raid on security guards transferring wages from one part of the site to others for distribution to the workers. In the course of the raid, shots were fired by the criminals, slightly wounding two of the security guards. James Kennedy was on duty at the main gate of the complex that evening. Hearing the shots, so knowing that the raiders were armed, he nevertheless stood his ground in the gateway and tackled the first criminal to reach the gate. The others came to the raider's aid, however, and Kennedy was assaulted and beaten with the barrels of the sawn-off shotguns.

Despite his injuries, Kennedy did what he could to prevent the gang from escaping in their getaway van. As he tried to approach the van, however, he was killed by two shots fired by the gang member sitting in the front seat.

An electric locomotive was named *James Kennedy GC* in 1981.

RAILWAY ANIMALS

Horses

As we've seen, horses were used to haul wagons along some form of tracked way for centuries before the invention of the moving steam locomotive. And even in early steam days, horses continued to work many trains. Some lines continued to use horse traction for a surprisingly long time – generally when it was found that the economies of using locomotives didn't stack up. The passenger service on the short branch of the Carlisle to Silloth line from Drumburgh to Port Carlisle was operated using horse traction right up to 1914. Quite apart from exceptional situations like that, railway companies kept huge numbers of horses – pre-motor vehicles they were used to deliver goods as well as shunting goods wagons at stations. Provided only one or two wagons needed to be moved, a horse proved more flexible than a locomotive, was available at any time and only needed to be handled by one person. Over 9,000 railway horses passed to the British Transport Commission on nationalization in 1948 and the final example of horses used for shunting railway wagons on the day-to-day railway was at Newmarket, Suffolk, as late as 1967.

Cats and Dogs

The station cat was a staple character at many stations – good for keeping the local mouse population in check. Many large stations also had dogs with charity boxes on their backs. They would be sent off to wander at will in the hope that kind-hearted passengers would dip into their pockets. The charity was normally something railway-related – for example the Southern Railwaymens' Home for Orphans at Woking

Station Jim

or the Great Western Railway Widows' and Orphans' Fund.

Some of these dogs became familiar and well-loved features of the stations they worked at and after they died some were stuffed and put on display at their former stamping grounds. There used to be examples at Wimbledon and at Waterloo in London and you can still see 'Station Jim' at Slough in Berkshire, secure in his case on platform 5. He had been brought to the station when just three months old to serve as a collector, and quickly became popular when he was taught to bark whenever money was placed in his box. The citation on his glass case describes some of his other tricks:

> *He would sit up and beg, or lie down and 'die'; he could make a bow when asked, or stand up on his hind legs. He would get up and sit in a chair and look quite at home with a pipe in his mouth and cap on his head. He would express his feelings in a very noisy manner when he heard any music. If anyone threw a lighted match or a piece of lighted paper on the ground he would extinguish it with a growl. If a ladder was placed against the wall he would climb it. He would play leap frog with the boys; he would escort them off the station if told to do so, but would never bite them. At a St. John Ambulance Examination held at this station he laid down on one of the stretchers and allowed himself to be bandaged up with the rest of the 'injured'.*

Station Jim died suddenly in his harness on the platform on 19 November 1896 and several Slough residents and station staff donated money to have his body preserved.

TAMA, THE STATIONMASTER CAT

At the end of June 2015, in Japan, thousands of people attended the funeral of a cat. The Kishigawa line in western Japan had been losing money – as part of cutbacks, human staff had been removed from stations but at Kishi, a former stray cat called Tama had been created honorary stationmaster. Thousands of people then began visiting the station to see this most unusual member of staff, who had been given a peaked cap to wear as a symbol of her authority, changing the fortunes of the line. On her death, at the age of 16, Tama was given the title of Honorary Eternal Stationmaster and enshrined as a goddess.

Pigeons and Hawks

Pigeons, to many people, are nothing but avian pests, befouling anywhere they land. To pigeon-fanciers, however, they are something completely different – fine racing animals that can find their way home from anywhere in the country. In the heyday of the railways, 'pigeon specials' were run across the country – long trains of pigeon vans full of birds taken far from their homes and released once they reached their destinations. For those who are more inclined to view pigeons as pests, the good news is that rail companies regularly employ hawk handlers, to fly the predatory birds around stations and frighten away the resident pigeons.

THE RAILWAY HOBBY

PUBLICATIONS

FOR AS LONG AS there have been railways and trains, there have been people fascinated by them. And whenever people are interested in something, other people will produce material to sell to them.

In 1897, the first issue of *The Railway Magazine* was published in London. A monthly publication, it is still published today and remains one of the most popular railway publications in the country. Other periodicals have entered the market since the *RM* started, both in the UK and around the world. Today's enthusiasts can choose between magazines dealing with steam trains, general nostalgia, modern trains or a mix of all three.

Trainspotting and Bashing

Some railway enthusiasts indulge in trainspotting, in which they try to see as many examples as possible of their chosen subject of interest, whether types of locomotive, carriages or wagons. In the UK, loco-spotting saw its heyday from the late 1940s – publisher Ian Allan produced handy books (the *ABCs*) showing all of the locomotives in their individual classes, making it easy to record which examples you had seen. These guides, in their modern forms, are still available today. Ian Allan died on 28 June 2015, on the eve of his ninety-third birthday.

Bashing is another form of the hobby, involving travelling over as much of a rail network as possible or travelling behind as many individual locomotives as possible.

HERITAGE ORGANIZATIONS

For a less intense heritage experience, dozens of organizations around the world have preserved running lines, locomotives and rolling stock to offer a taste of rail travel in the old days. And many countries have official railway museums, offering the chance for people to get right up close to artefacts in a safe environment.

CONCLUSION

S
O THERE WE ARE – a bit of a breathless jog through railway history. Railways have been around for nearly 200 years – they have spanned the globe, conquering terrain and climate, and despite rumours of their decline have gone from strength to strength, providing efficient methods of mass transportation in and between cities, and now moving into major and competitive players even across vast distances in Asia. They have helped create cities, open up continents, even fix time itself. And even whilst writing this book, news came of a new world speed record in Japan. Who knows what exciting developments are yet to come?

BIBLIOGRAPHY

Atterbury, Paul; *Life along the Line* (David & Charles, 2010)

Bryan, Tim; *The Great Western Railway* (Ian Allan, 2010)

Dendy-Marshall, C.F.; *History of the Southern Railway* (Ian Allan, 1968)

Dickens, Charles; *American Notes for General Circulation* (Penguin Books, first published 1842)

Dickens, Charles; *Dombey & Son* (Penguin Books, first published 1848)

Lambert, Anthony; *Lambert's Railway Miscellany* (Ebury Press, 2010)

Manley, Deborah (ed); *The Railway Anthology* (Trailblazer, 2014)

Marsh, Philip; *The Age of the Train* (Carlton Books, 2011)

Quinn, Tom; *Memories of Steam* (David & Charles, 2008)

Robertson, Kevin; *The Leader Project* (Oxford Publishing Company, 2007)

Roden, Andrew; *Great Western Railway* (Aurum, 2011)

Simmons, Jack and Biddle, Gordon (eds); *The Oxford Companion to British Railway History* (Oxford University Press, 1997)

Tolstoy, Leo; *Anna Karenina* (Oxford University Press, first published 1877)

Whitehouse, Patrick and Thomas, David St John; *LNER 150* (David & Charles, 2002)

Wolmar, Christian; *Blood, Iron and Gold* (Atlantic Books, 2010)

Wolmar, Christian; *Fire and Steam* (Atlantic Books, 2008)

Wolmar, Christian; *The Iron Road* (Dorling Kindersley, 2014)

Wolmar, Christian; *The Subterranean Railway* (Atlantic Books, 2009)

Wragg, David; *LMS Handbook* (Haynes Publishing, 2010)

Zola, Émile; *La Bête Humaine* (Penguin Books, first published 1890)

Internet Links

Amtrak: http://www.amtrak.com/home

California high-speed rail authority: http://www.hsr.ca.gov/

Canadian Pacific: http://www.cpr.ca/en/about-cp/our-history

China-Russia high-speed rail link: http://rt.com/business/225131-russia-china-speed-railway/

Track destroying machine: http://rarehistoricalphotos.com/german-troops-use-schwellenpflug-destroy-rail-tracks-withdrawing-soviet-territory-1944/

PICTURE ACKNOWLEDGEMENTS

Locomotion No. 1 (page 16): illustration by Aubrey Smith

Isambard Kingdom Brunel (page 20): illustration by Aubrey Smith

Thames Tunnel Construction Shield (page 21): Clipart.com

Clifton Suspension Bridge (page 22): illustration by Aubrey Smith

Interior of a Pullman car (page 31): © duncan1890/iStock

Mountain train in front of the Matterhorn peak (page 40): © Olimpiu Pop/Shutterstock

Workers on the Panama Railroad *c.* 1910, from the James Gordon Steese Papers (page 45): Courtesy of Archives and Special Collections, Dickinson College, Carlisle, PA, USA

Union Pacific Railroad (page 47): map by Aubrey Smith

The Harvey Girls, 1945 (page 51): © Metro-Goldwyn-Mayer/ Getty Images

The Canadian Pacific Railway Trans-Canada, near Lake Louise, Alberta, 1927 (page 53): Canada. Dept. of Interior/Library and Archives Canada/PA-049791

The Trans-Siberian Railway (page 63): map by Aubrey Smith

Steam train underground, 1875 (page 74): © HultonArchive/iStock

Construction of the Metropolitan District Railway, London, *c.* 1867 (page 76): Science & Society Picture Library/ Getty Images

Magnus Volk's Daddy-Long-Legs (page 79): illustration by Aubrey Smith

Moscow metro station Novoslobodskaya (page 92):
© Viacheslav Lopatin/Shutterstock

Curve at Brooklyn Terminal, Brooklyn Bridge, New York, 1898 (page 94): Geo. P. Hall & Son photographers, N.Y./ Library of Congress, Prints & Photographs Division [LC-USZ62-5414]

Festungsbahn (page 98): Photo by JD, distributed under licence CC BY-SA 3.0

Japanese magnetic levitation train (page 110): Photograph by Kiyoshi Ota/Bloomberg via Getty Images

Landscape with Carriage and Train in the Background by Vincent van Gogh, 1890 (page 125): The Yorck Project: 10,000 Meisterwerke der Malerei

Mallard (page 149): illustration by Aubrey Smith

Flying Scotsman (page 152): illustration by Aubrey Smith

Station Jim (page 174): illustration by Aubrey Smith

Tama (page 176): illustration by Aubrey Smith

ACKNOWLEDGEMENTS

Many people encouraged me to write this book. Huge thanks to my mother, Micas Saxton; to Kirsh and Gary, Isa, Ian and Natasha, Gabrielle and David; to Bea Carvalho and the entire team at Waterstones; to Alison Parker and Sally Wilks; to Gabby Nemeth my editor; to Louise Dixon and all of the staff at Michael O'Mara; to illustrator Aubrey Smith and cover designer Patrick Knowles.

INDEX